New Approaches to Decolonizing Fashion History and Period Styles

New Approaches to Decolonizing Fashion History and Period Styles: Re-Fashioning Pedagogies offers a wide array of inclusive, global, practical approaches for teaching costume and fashion history.

Costume designers, technicians, and historians have spent the last several years re-evaluating how they teach costume and fashion history, acknowledging the need to refocus the discourse to include a more global perspective. This book is a collection of pedagogical methods aimed to do just that, with an emphasis on easy reference, accessible activities, and rubrics, and containing a variety of ways to restructure the course. Each chapter offers a course description, syllabus calendar, course objectives, and learning outcomes, as well as sample activities from instructors across the country who have made major changes to their coursework. Using a combination of personal narratives, examples from their work, bibliographies of helpful texts, and student responses, contributors suggest a variety of ways to decolonize the traditionally Western-focused fashion history syllabus.

This collection of pedagogical approaches is intended to support and inspire instructors teaching costume design, costume history, fashion history, period styles, and other aesthetic histories in the arts.

Ashley Bellet is a professional costume designer and crafts artisan. She is an assistant professor of costume design at Purdue University in West Lafayette, Indiana, and secretary for the United States Institute for Theatre Technology (USITT).

New Approaches to Decolonizing Fashion History and Period Styles

Re-Fashioning Pedagogies

Edited by Ashley Bellet

NEW YORK AND LONDON

Cover image by Serge Mouangue

First published 2024
by Routledge
605 Third Avenue, New York, NY 10158

and by Routledge
4 Park Square, Milton Park, Abingdon, Oxon, OX14 4RN

Routledge is an imprint of the Taylor & Francis Group, an informa business

© 2024 selection and editorial matter, Ashley Bellet; individual chapters, the contributors

The right of Ashley Bellet to be identified as the author of the editorial material, and of the authors for their individual chapters, has been asserted in accordance with sections 77 and 78 of the Copyright, Designs and Patents Act 1988.

All rights reserved. No part of this book may be reprinted or reproduced or utilised in any form or by any electronic, mechanical, or other means, now known or hereafter invented, including photocopying and recording, or in any information storage or retrieval system, without permission in writing from the publishers.

Trademark notice: Product or corporate names may be trademarks or registered trademarks, and are used only for identification and explanation without intent to infringe.

ISBN: 978-1-032-23544-8 (hbk)
ISBN: 978-1-032-23542-4 (pbk)
ISBN: 978-1-003-27818-4 (ebk)

DOI: 10.4324/9781003278184

Typeset in Palatino
by Apex CoVantage, LLC

Contents

Cover Artist	*vii*
Notes on Contributors	*viii*
Acknowledgements	*xv*

	Introduction: New Perspectives and Taking Chances ASHLEY BELLET	1
1	Re-Fashioning Time: An Object-Based Approach to the History of Style SYDNEY MARESCA	7
2	Research Methods for Fashion History and Technology GRACE COCHRAN KEENAN	23
3	Conscious Fashion History CAMILLE BENDA	34
4	Fashion Forward: A History of Dress in Global Context JULIE LEAVITT LEARSON	45
5	Global Dress History for Undergraduate General Education ANASTASIA GOODWIN	71
6	Historic Costume and Décor Utilizing a People- and Place-Based Curriculum MAILE SPEETJENS AND MICHELLE BISBEE	83
7	An Abridged Clothing History in Four Construction Techniques LENA SANDS	102
8	Examining and Creating Connections in Costume History Through Cultural Intersections and Alternative Assessment Models SARAH MOSHER	120

9 Expanding and Deconstructing the Western Fashion History Ideology RAFAEL JAEN	140
10 Fashion and Costume: Global Adornment and Attire SARAH M. OLIVER	156
11 The March of History Gives Way to Flowers in a Field CHRIS MULLER	173
12 Activities for the Classroom	183
Project A: Worn History: Personal History Through Clothes DEBRA KRAJEC	184
Project B: Final Assignment: World Building BRENDA VAN DER WIEL	191
Project C: Historic Tools and Techniques: An Exercise in Material Culture Observation ASHLEY BELLET	200
Conclusion ASHLEY BELLET	205
Index	*207*

Cover Artist

Cameroon-born Serge Mouangue is a multimedia artist and designer currently residing in Paris, France. Through his use of sculpture, fiber arts, and industrial design, Mouangue combines cultural iconography to inspire conversations about identity. His vision of the '3rd aesthetic,' a world of exploratory design that transcends architecture, industry, and fashion, led him to establish *Wafrica* as the creative platform for his designs.

Mouangue's work explores cultural origins and identity by exploring human engagement with material objects such as costume, mask, and ritual objects. His process of design is united with his process of creation; his inspiration drives the realization of his work through experimentation and making. In an interview with WIPO, Mouangue describes how he ". . . focus[es] on building and changing the environment by creating a new narrative using things that we can touch, hear, smell and live with. Design is a way to tell a story through things that we can feel." By actively manipulating familiar symbols of individual cultures, Mouangue seeks to destabilize expectations and re-value the impact of change through globalization. His works are charged with the energy of encountering objects, just as he is driven by his inspiration with the material world. The cover photograph has been graciously shared by Serge Mouangue, and is one of the first pieces from his project *Kimono* following a residency in Japan. The project has been shown at the Fesman festival in Dakar, the Museum of Art and Design in New York, the Museum der Kulturen, Basel, the Etnografiska museet, Stockholm, Tokyo, the Nishi Hongan-ji temple in Kyoto, TICAD VII, Nairobi, 2017, the Maison de la Culture du Japon a Paris, and the Victoria and Albert Museum exhibition on kimono in 2020.

Notes on Contributors

Ashley Bellet is an assistant professor of costume design at Purdue University and a professional designer and crafts artisan. She received her MFA from the University of Memphis and BAs in theatre and English from Sewanee and is completing her PhD in interdisciplinary theatre studies from UW Madison. Ashley serves as the secretary for USITT and has served on the board of directors as the vice president for commissions; she is also the associate editor for education for theatre design and technology (TD&T). She is an active member of and presenter with KCACTF, SETC's Theater Symposium, ATCA, Critical Costume, ATHE, and USITT and a fellow of the Society for Experiential Education (SEE). Ashley has worked at the Santa Fe Opera, Playhouse on the Square, and American Players Theatre, among others. As a designer and craftsperson, Ashley's research leans heavily on practice-based methodologies (PaR) and pedagogy for the design classroom. Combining material culture studies, aesthetic theory, and object agency, she constructs costumes that examine the architecture and energy created in the space between the body and the costume. Her work with USITT highlights her design pedagogy, integrating hands-on experiences with a deeper level of aesthetic research constructed outside the production process.

With 25 years of experience working in theatre, film, television, and commercials, Camille Benda has enjoyed the process of supporting directors, producers, and actors in realizing their creative vision through costume design, having worked with actors across the globe like Elizabeth McGovern, Julie Delpy, Eve Hewson, Ben Whishaw, J. K. Simmons, Sam Claflin, and Ellie Kemper. Camille's research-led design approach started with a love of art history and languages, evolving into a passion for character and script interpretation once she discovered costume design for theatre. Her recent projects include costume design for *Bad Sisters*, the 10-part Apple TV+ series starring Sharon Horgan and Daryl McCormack and *Bernhard/Hamlet* at the Geffen Theater directed by Sarna Lapine (postponed during the pandemic). Recent films include *The Last Manhunt* (2022), produced by Jason Momoa and set in 1907 frontier California, starring Christian Camargo, Lily Gladstone, and Raoul Trujillo. Camille is also the head of costume design in the School of Theatre at California Institute of the Arts. She has an MFA in theatre design from the Yale School of Drama, and a Masters of Art from the Courtauld Institute in the history of dress. Her first print book, *Dressing the Resistance*, published by Princeton Architectural Press in 2021, celebrates the role of clothing, costume, and nudity in activism and protest. While working in the film industry across the US and Europe, Camille enjoys presenting talks on dress history and costume design at numerous institutions, including the Victoria & Albert Museum, the Costume Society, Stanford University, UC Berkeley, SDSU, and Arts Center College of Design. Camille was invited to be a guest speaker at the 2022 Jeddah Book Fair in Saudi Arabia and has moderated panels for Disney Studios and the American Theatrical Costume Association.

Anastasia Goodwin was born and raised in the former Soviet Union, in the city of Saratov. An opportunity to participate in a high school exchange program with the United States brought Anastasia to Texas, where she ended up in the theatre class and after-school performance program. This experience led her to ultimately pursue a theatre degree in the United States. She majored in costume design at the University of Central Missouri. After graduation and an apprenticeship at the Santa Fe Opera, Anastasia was able to share her skills with the company of the Saratov State Drama Theatre until finally emigrating to the US and moving to the Pacific Northwest. There, she worked as a stitcher in several union houses (Village Theatre, ACT, Seattle Opera, Pacific Northwest Ballet) while pursuing design opportunities at smaller companies. Eventually, Anastasia completed her MFA studies in costume design at the University of Washington School of Drama. After a few years as the assistant costume department manager of Seattle Rep, Anastasia decided it was time to focus on her long-held goal of becoming an educator. This brought her to Saint Mary's University of Minnesota, where her class Dress and Fashion: Global History and Impact was developed. Her research on the subject has been presented at conferences for both USITT and CSA, highlighting the need for further in-depth scholarly exploration. Anastasia is excited to begin her doctoral studies at Vanderbilt University's Peabody College.

Rafael Jaen (pronounced HA-en) is a professional costume designer, professor, and author. His film, TV, and theatre design work has received multiple accolades. He received the Kennedy Center Golden Medallion for Excellence in Theatre Education, the Salem State University Center for Creative and Performing Arts Life Achievement in the Arts Award, and the UMass Boston Manning Prize for Teaching Excellence. He also received a Joseph P. Healey research grant titled Secession, Entrepreneurship and Haute Couture in the USA During the Civil War Years and a Mellon Grant High-Impact Humanities Initiative to develop the course Enlivening Identities

Through Dress. Additionally, Mr. Jaen is a USITT fellow, and he has served in multiple national roles at USITT and KCACTF. Jaen is the performing arts department chair and a full professor of theatre at UMass Boston. He is the author of *SHOWCASE* by Focal Press and *Digital Costume Design and Collaboration* by Focal Press/Routledge. He also co-wrote two chapters for the book *Fashioning Horror: Dressing to Kill on Screen and Literature* by Bloomsbury. He is the main editor of the Backstage series, a publishing partnership between USITT and Routledge.

Grace Cochran Keenan is an assistant professor of technology at Kent State University as well as a freelance tailor and draper. Grace received her Master of Fine Arts in costume design/technology from Pennsylvania State University and her Bachelor of Fine Arts in theatre design/production from Kent State University. Since receiving her MFA, she has worked as a freelance draper and tailor in the Cleveland area, with credits at the Glimmerglass Festival, Carnegie Mellon University, Great Lakes Theatre, the Cleveland Playhouse, the Idaho Shakespeare Festival, Baldwin-Wallace University, and the Porthouse Theatre. She has over 50 credits to her name as a draper and tailor, including *Candide*, *Deathtrap*, *Sweeney Todd*, *Intimate Apparel*, and *The Plague of Venice*. During this time, she also served as adjunct faculty at Kent State University, prior to joining the faculty full time in 2018. Her courses include History of Costume and Textile for Theatre, Flat Patterning for Theatre, Draping for the Theatre I, Draping for the Theatre II, Basic Costume Construction, and Costume Production Management. In addition to her work as a tailor and draper, Grace's research interests are the importance of making in the human experience through the history of dress and crafts and flipped learning as it applies to the arts. Currently, she is working on a five-year study on flipped learning and its effect on student stress in a studio-based classroom.

Debra Krajec is an associate professor of theatre arts at Marquette University in Milwaukee. Since 1984, she has served as a costume designer and stage director for the theatre program. She received her MFA from Texas Christian University in 1982 and has worked professionally as a costume designer, a director, and an actress. At Marquette, Debra teaches Costume Design, History of Clothing, Stage Directing, Auditioning and Career Prep, and other courses. In 2011, she received a John P. Raynor, S.J., Faculty Award for Teaching Excellence. Debra has designed costumes for Milwaukee Repertory Theatre, Milwaukee Chamber Theatre, First Stage Milwaukee, Renaissance Theaterworks, Next Act Theatre, Retro Productions in NYC, St. Michael's Playhouse in Vermont, and Casa Mañana Playhouse in Texas. In the summer of 2022, she was production designer for a feature-length film entitled *DIFFRACTION* produced by Heron Media Films. She is very active in the United States Institute for Theatre Technology, where she is a fellow of the institute, a member of the board of directors, and past costume design and technology commissioner. She is a member of Actors' Equity Association.

Julie Leavitt Learson is a member of Fairfield University's theatre program faculty, where she teaches a variety of theatre courses. She is also costume director of Fairfield University's production company, designing and executing costumes, hair, and makeup for university productions; managing the costume shop; and mentoring students in costume design and tech. She was previously an assistant professor of English at Westfield State College, where she designed costume and lighting. In addition to her teaching career, Julie has been a long-time artist in residence at Shakesperience Productions in Waterbury, Connecticut, a company dedicated to bringing live performances and interactive workshops to classrooms and communities around the state, kindling a love of theatre in young audiences. She has also designed costumes professionally for several theatre companies in the Chicago area, including the Organic Touchstone Theatre, Emerald City Children's Theatre, Pyewackett Theatre, and Frump Tucker Theater Company. She also served the assistant to the costume designer at the Goodman Theatre of Chicago, where she helped create the costume spaces at their Dearborn Street location, and assistant costume designer for Lookingglass Theatre Company. Julie earned her MFA in costume design at Northwestern University, with a secondary area in lighting design. She is a member of Phi Beta Kappa and Phi Kappa Phi, as well as USITT, the Costume Society, the Costume Society of America, and ATCA. A firm believer that theatre is a natural empathy maker and conscious expander, Julie strives to produce meaningful, passionate, and empowering art for audiences and collaborators alike.

Sydney Maresca is a visiting assistant professor of theatre at Williams College. Her design work has been seen on Broadway, cable television, and around the world. Notable projects include the Broadway premiere of *The Cottage*, directed by Jason Alexander; the Broadway premiere and North American tour of *The Lighting Thief: The Percy Jackson Musical*; the Broadway and London premieres of the award-winning play *Hand to God*; and *Real Enemies* at the Brooklyn Academy of Music's Next Wave Festival. She is currently pursuing a master's degree in decorative arts, design history, and material culture at the Bard Graduate Center with a focus on clothing and textiles in the early American Northeast that speak to indigenous and immigrant encounters, craft, labor, and women's roles in their communities. Sydney has an MFA from NYU's Tisch Department of Design for Stage and Film and a BA from Sarah Lawrence College.

Sarah Mosher is an assistant professor of costume design and technology at Baylor University. Sarah is interested in the critical area of sustainability of both materials and labor in theatre practice. She has worked professionally as a costume designer for theatre, opera, film, and dance in Seattle and in Central Texas. Her work has encompassed interdisciplinary-devised work, and she has a passion for the dramaturgical work inherent in theatrical design. In academia, Sarah is invested in the implementation of critical pedagogy practices and expanding student experience to encompass embodied learning.

Chris Muller received his BA in studio art from the University of California, Davis, and his MFA in set design and art direction from New York University. Recent design work includes art director and lead designer for the Sustainability Pavilion for the Dubai World Expo 2020; master planning for the Philadelphia Zoo; costume renderings for *Ready Player One*, a feature film directed by Stephen Spielberg; and period illustrations for *Hostiles*, a feature directed by Scott Cooper; and projection content and design for *The Summer King*, Pittsburgh Opera, *The Golden Cockerel*, Santa Fe Opera, and *The 12 Days of Christmas*, Radio City Christmas spectacular. Chris is the principal at Chris Muller Design, which creates museum exhibits and experiences. Recent projects include *Unrestricted Warfare: The Last Mission of the U.S.S. Tang* for the National World War II Museum, New Orleans and exhibits for the Museum for African Art, the Whitney Museum of American Art, the Yale University Art Gallery, the Miami Children's Museum, and the American Craft Museum. He was the lead designer for the Rock and Roll Hall of Fame (redux), the Muhammad Ali Center, the National Track and Field Hall of Fame, and the College Basketball Experience and Hall of Fame. Corporate clients have included Sapphire Software, Time/Warner, Clinique, and Sony. Theatre design collaborations include the Alvin Ailey Dance Company, the Juilliard Opera, the Measured Breaths Opera Company, the Atlantic Stage Company, Shapiro and Smith Dance, East Coast Artists, the Welsh National Dance Company, the Contemporary Legends Theater of Taiwan, and Laurie Anderson's multimedia world tour *Scenes from the Nerve Bible*. Chris also illustrated the recently published children's book *The Griffin and the Dinosaur* for National Geographic.

Sarah M. Oliver is assistant professor of costume technology and design at the University of Michigan at Ann Arbor. Previously, she taught costume technology at University of Missouri-Kansas City and was the senior lecturer of costume technology at the Hong Kong Academy for Performing

Arts. Oliver has designed and built costumes in the United States for theatres coast to coast – from the Los Angeles Opera to the New York City Opera. She has built costumes for drama, film, dance, opera, and musical theatre productions for designers in South Africa, England, Spain, Hong Kong, Canada, China, and the Bahamas. Over the course of her career, Oliver has worked in almost all levels of costuming – as a designer, assistant, maker, costume shop manager, wig maker, fabric dyer, wardrobe supervisor, and dresser. While she has dedicated her professional career to designing, building, and teaching the art of costuming, Oliver continues to indulge in her first love – the study of textiles and weaving. She has traveled and worked internationally in China, Hong Kong, and Japan, where she immersed herself in traditional weaving, embroidery, and dyeing arts.

Lena Sands is an award-winning practitioner and teacher of costume design. In her costume design and technology courses at Los Angeles Mission College and Verdugo Hills High School, Lena harnesses the students' innate curiosity to help them develop the technical, socio-emotional, communication, and research skills to position their design work within a global visual matrix. Lena previously taught fashion design at the Los Angeles County High School of the Arts (LACHSA), which was named the number-one arts high school in the country during her time there. As a costume designer for theatre, installation, dance, and opera, Lena uses a variety of materials and methods to create bold and distinctive visuals and collaborates with ensembles and communities to investigate bodies, histories, and the divine. Her work in devised theatre, including her process and renderings, is highlighted in Routledge's book *Creating Costumes for Devised Theatre* by Kyla Kazuschyk (2023). Lena's notable costume designs include SITI company's *Bacchae* (BAM, Guthrie, Getty Villa); Pat Benetar's *Invincible: The Musical* (The Wallis); and Jennifer Koh and Davóne Tines's *Everything Rises* (Royce Hall, BAM). Other favorite collaborators include Critical Mass Performance Group, Four Larks, Cornerstone Theater, Naked Empire Buffon, and Heidi Duckler Dance. Her designs for *Venus* by Suzan-Lori Parks were displayed at the State Historical Museum in Moscow as part of the exhibition Innovative Costume of the 21st Century: The Next Generation. Lena has a BFA in design and production from University of Michigan and an MFA in design for performance from California Institute of the Arts.

Maile Speetjens received her BFA from Emerson College and her MFA from the University of Georgia, Athens, and serves as assistant professor of costumes, hair, and makeup at the University of Hawai'i at Mānoa. Maile's work in costumes has spanned from Boston to Hawai'i and in between. Recent work includes *Aloha Attire* (Kumu Kahua Theatre, Honolulu),

Twelfth Night (Lyric Repertory), *Conversion of Ka'ahumanu* (Kumu Kahua Theatre, Honolulu), and *'Au'a 'Ia: Holding On* (UH Mānoa Hana Keaka). Current research interests include empathy-centered pedagogical strategies, decolonizing approaches to design work and course construction, Hana Keaka (Hawaiian medium theatre), Hana Lima No'eau (Hawaiian adornment and craftwork), and new strategies in digital draping technology. Maile serves as the design, technology, and management chair of the Kennedy Center American College Theatre Festival, Region 8.

Brenda Van der Wiel serves as head of the performing arts design program for the University of Utah. Most recently, she designed *The Sound of Music* for the Utah Shakespeare Festival. She designs regularly for both the department and Pioneer Theatre. Recent shows for Pioneer Theatre include *Scapin, Fireflies, Mary Stuart, Sweeney Todd, Fences, Outside Mullingar, Alabama Story, Rent,* and *Emma*. Brenda has also designed extensively for the Alabama Shakespeare Festival. In recent years, she has designed *Annie, The Glass Menagerie, A Midsummer Night's Dream, The Little Mermaid, Mary Poppins, The Great Gatsby, Macbeth, Merry Wives of Windsor,* and *The Count of Monte Cristo*. Designs for the Utah Shakespeare Festival include *Mary Poppins, A Midsummer Night's Dream,* and *Treasure Island*. She has also worked at the Seattle Opera and the Santa Fe Opera.

Acknowledgements

This book is a collection of hours of research from incredibly generous colleagues across the country, to whom I will be eternally grateful for their time, their ideas, and their willingness to share so much. The idea of the book began as part of the American Theatrical Costume Association, ATCA, to whom we owe the chance to gather our ideas together. To Chloe Chapin and Christianne Myers, the founding members of ATCA, we thank you for raising this discussion and bringing it national focus.

Introduction

New Perspectives and Taking Chances

Ashley Bellet

In the spring of 2020, costume designers, technicians, and educators from across the country gathered online for the first official conference for the American Theatrical Costume Association (ATCA). The brainchild of Chloe Chapin and Christianne Myers, this event began with two goals: Connecting professionals across the country and addressing critical, contemporary topics of interest across the field. This first conference focused on the necessity of decolonizing our syllabi – breaking down reliance on a canon of Western aesthetic reference, escaping from the pedagogical methods we had ourselves been taught, and garnering resources and support from our colleagues across the US. Ultimately, we came together to talk about changing what and how we teach.

In the subsequent years, ATCA has grown to become a stand-alone online resource, and the annual conferences in 2021 and 2022 focused on topics like power dynamics and leadership in the workplace and the links between pedagogical adaptation and mental health. Nevertheless, there remained a consistent thread of conversation surrounding the changing pedagogies of teaching fashion history. So many of us relied on survey-style courses that mimicked traditional art history formats, focusing on Western and European silhouettes, politics, and economic trends that ultimately influenced contemporary fashion.

There have been quiet discussion and admiration for those who changed their courses; however, many of us hesitated to make substantial change for a few reasons. One, many programs have built their seasons and curriculum on the knowledge of Western theatre. We felt an obligation to teach students things we knew they'd use in the immediate future. Two, classes like fashion history and period styles have become the milestone courses – expectations of memorization, research, and endless vocabulary have earned them the reputation of "get through this, get through anything." Three, time. The time it takes to prep any class, much less to make substantial change to a class, is . . . substantial. Dramatic change to a future course on top of teaching, producing, and serving the university is an exercise in priorities, especially when prep for that class in the first place (when doing it the same way you've done it before) is mammoth. Imagine trying to engage with all of aesthetic history, around the world, in sixteen weeks or less. The pressure is enough to intimidate anyone.

The Scope of the Text

The most common theme you will find is that of change – dramatic, sweeping, and intentional. While several contributors took advantage of the last few years' disruption to take drastic steps in their teaching approaches, several others have been doggedly pursuing this project for years. Some approach the change in a single swoop, others as a step-by-step scaffolding of individual pedagogical elements. There are no two educational situations that are the same – student makeup, course objectives, curricular process, and departmental expectations are just a few of the pieces that make up how each contributor has gone about making change. There are advantages to having accessed this moment of reflection and evolution; however, there are also very real stumbling blocks our contributors have discovered in their work. Student expectations of the material, colleagues' fear of new approaches, and the simple truth that the amount of time we have to research and offer this information in no way matches the amount of aesthetic history we are trying to teach – these are a few of the recurring moments encountered here.

This book is structured to offer a variety of ways to integrate change into your fashion history and period styles courses. Authors come from a variety of schools, both university and high school levels and large and small departments; their courses cover majors and general education, fashion, and architecture and serve a wide variety of student populations. Chapters have been grouped according to the broad themes of their courses, and there is a section containing individual, specific projects to integrate on a micro level. Each chapter outlines course objectives, or the broad goals of the instructor, as well as the course learning outcomes – the measurable skills or techniques students will learn and be graded on. Finally, there is a bibliography for those texts and articles most referenced internally that can be found in the appendices of this book.

The combination of lack of resources and support is endemic – this volume offers a tangible reference to the work our colleagues are doing at a variety of levels, with respect to the complex and unique qualities of this type of course. The best support we have is that which we offer to each other – this is a book of your colleagues' work with content that immediately pertains to this course in particular.

The first section of the book, with contributions by Sydney Maresca and Grace Cochran Keenan, shows a desire to reframe the work of learning from memorization to knowledge finding. Maresca offers an outline that reorders the concept of historical evolutions, building on her students' intuitive strengths as a foundation for research methodology. Keenan similarly focuses on students' research skills but integrates a maker-influenced thread of projects that ties together content and active learning.

The second section focuses on how historical power relationships have affected not only what we know but also how we know about the history of fashion and aesthetics. Camille Benda constructs a firm framework for the work of the conscious fashion student, looking to movements of resistance and power struggles and how those directed fashion both within and beyond mainstream consciousness. Julie Learson focuses on themes of fashion as personal expression through resistance, dress codes, and sustainability. In her chapter, Global Dress History for Undergraduate General Education, Anastasia Goodwin integrates the themes of her university's general education requirements with those of her global fashion history class, concentrating on themes of global and local social justice and sustainability.

The third section embraces the maker and their immediate cultural influences. Maile Speetjens utilizes her local resources, artisans, and cultural background to explore how learning about one place on a deep and personal level models the practice of exploring any culture. Lena Sands combines the necessary analysis of shape and form through the eyes of the maker with a view of how those shapes evolved to serve individual cultural styles.

In the fourth section, Sarah Mosher combines the tracing of cultural intersections, trade, and social justice with a pedagogical approach that breaks down traditional grading practices. Using a similar approach to cultural intersections, Rafael Jaen investigates activities, rituals, and events that cross the boundaries between cultures and societies. Sarah M. Oliver correlates and highlights design and practices from a variety of global cultures, combining her experiences with her research to highlight traditional practices and crafts. Both Jaen and Oliver break their courses into modules, allowing them to inject or adapt certain sections as needed or desired. Chris Muller re-envisions the content itself as a field from which he and the students may choose themes and discover correlations, recognizing that the field is ever changing. His approach moves far beyond visual history or period styles to incorporate economic, political, and social histories as well.

Across the subsequent chapters, several pedagogical themes appear. Some may be familiar; others may be somewhat new. One strong theme found throughout, however, is the idea that the professor is a knowledgeable source but not an expert. By refocusing the students' work on finding and developing knowledge instead of simply receiving knowledge, the role of the professor is that of facilitator. In reality, there is little possibility that a single person may retain every bit of aesthetic history from around the world, so by breaking down the concept of the "expert," we empower students to discover, release pressure on the professor to know everything, and deconstruct the hierarchy of knowledge giver and knowledge receiver.

Supporting this idea, you will find that many of these courses rely on research-based teaching methods. Forays into archives both on and off campus, student-led research presentations, and an emphasis on vertical instead of horizontal learning permeate most of these courses, further directing students into the role of knowledge gatherers. This approach reflects an emphasis on Bloom's taxonomy, in which higher-order thinking employs analysis and evaluation. While Bloom's has been around for many, many years in the field, there are newer, more complex revisions that offer more detail and include digital learning applications as well. (See Figure 0.1)

The flipped classroom is based heavily on the concepts of active and passive learning. Passive learning, or the intake of information (reading, surveying, memorization) is performed outside the classroom in order to allow active learning to occur inside the classroom. Active learning includes physical engagement, hands-on learning, analysis, and other higher-level learning goals on Bloom's taxonomy.

Another trend you will find is that of looking directly to objects for information gathering, rather than focusing on images or slides. This approach embraces the growing interest in material culture, or the objects that make up our social, cultural, and aesthetic history. Objects carry an agency and identity both within and beyond their respective histories and looking directly to things like garments, tools, and original documents brings students closer to the styles they are studying. This pedagogical approach is directly related to what is traditionally recognized as hands-on learning and is often integrated with acquiring skills or practicing traditional methods of construction. Hands-on learning fuses the physical experience with the metacognitive nature of understanding history in the context of our current perspectives. It embraces not only "doing" but also "doing" and reflection on what is done.

Figure 0.1 Bloom's taxonomy: A re-envisioned, three-dimensional view that includes more complex ways of looking at each learned skill.

Source: Heer, Rex. "TeachThought." June 19, 2023, https://www.teachthought.com/critical-thinking/blooms-taxonomy-model-3d/.

Finally, you will find a burgeoning interest in interdisciplinary learning and experiences. These courses also integrate visual and experiential events, discussion, writing, creation, and reflection. Connections with community events, correlations between clothing and politics, sociological and anthropological research, and art history references are apparent across these courses. As most of us know, the content of a period styles or fashion history course is easily applicable to many academic subjects, and these contributors highlight how and when these interdisciplinary moments have enhanced their course content and structure.

You will also find that many of the contributors use the same or similar texts, all of which are quite different from the traditional Western-centered texts many of us learned from. Books about political resistance, global fashion, and how to read particular garments are the most common, with additions of contemporary academic articles and texts about specific cultures and practices. These once again highlight the interest in vertical (specific, deep learning on a topic) rather than horizontal (broad, survey-style learning across many topics) learning in an upper-level course in aesthetic history. Once again, the emphasis is on teaching the student good practices in research and knowledge accumulation, rather than feeding facts for memorization.

Perhaps the best approach we may offer overall is to ask the questions – not to have the answers. When we move away from the persona of "the expert on high" we model the act of discovery for our students. We refocus our courses to examine research practices, offering students guidance and autonomy in their own learning. We empower the students with a thirst for discovery that extends beyond a semester, a classroom, or a discipline.

1

Re-Fashioning Time

An Object-Based Approach to the History of Style

Sydney Maresca

Course Description

The history of style is the history of humanity. This year-long course uses an object-based approach to explore the meaning of style in historical dress, architecture, and décor. Beginning with how we think about and communicate ideas of style today, we work our way back through time in reverse-chronological order, exploring the stories of human experience that are told through spaces, objects, and dress. History of Style 1 begins with the present day and works back to the start of the eighteenth century. History of Style 2 picks up at the early eighteenth century and works back through time and geographies to the prehistoric period. Students build research and visual analysis skills, developing an understanding of period through objects and material culture. In this course, students are actively researching with digital media, print media, and objects using sources on the internet and in libraries, museums, archives, and more.

> School: Montclair State University
> Department: Theatre and Dance
> Level: Undergraduate Design and Technology students
> Class Size: 12–15 students
> Class Format: Online and Synchronous, Two Semesters

DOI: 10.4324/9781003278184-2

Texts or Core Materials:

Tiné, Hal. *Essentials of Period Style*, Routledge, 2015.

Weber, Susan and Kirkham, Pat, ed. *History of Design: Decorative Arts and Material Culture, 1400–2000*, Yale University Press, 2013.

Types of Access Needed: Computer with camera and microphone, access to the internet and the university library, digital camera (can be the camera on your phone)

Course Objectives and Learning Outcomes:
- Develop visual literacy for identifying period based on clothing, spaces, and objects;
- Build skills for researching images and objects across a range of sources;
- Practice object-based analysis; and
- Use the history of dress, architecture, and décor as a framework to interrogate world history.

Table 1.1 History of Style 1, Syllabus Calendar

History of Style 1		
Duration	**Learning Modules**	**Activities – In Class**
Week 1	What Is Style?	Syllabus and Learning Goals Research Citations
Week 2	What Is Architecture?	Visual Literacy: Contemporary People, Spaces, and Things Building Sources: the Internet
Week 3	What Is Clothing?	Visual Literacy: Building a Period Building Sources: Magazines
Week 4	What Is History?	Visual Literacy: The Early 2000s Building Sources: Image Databases
Week 5	2000 → 1970	Visual Literacy: Late 20th Century Building Sources: Secondary Sources
Week 6	1970 → 1930	Visual Literacy: Mid-20th Century Building Sources: Newspapers
Week 7	1930 → 1900	Visual Literacy: Early 20th Century Building Sources: Historical Societies

History of Style 1		
Duration	Learning Modules	Activities – In Class
Week 8	1900 → 1870	Visual Literacy: Late 19th Century Building Sources: Primary Texts
Week 9	1870 → 1840	Visual Literacy: Mid-19th Century Building Sources: Museums
Week 10	Research Plans	Research Individual Meetings to Discuss Projects
Week 11	1840 → 1800	Visual Literacy: Early 19th Century Building Sources: Archives
Week 12	1800 → 1770	Visual Literacy: Late 18th Century Building Sources: Archaeology
Week 13	1770 → 1750	Visual Literacy: Mid-18th Century Building Sources: Historical Archaeology
Week 14	1750 → 1700	Visual Literacy: Early 18th Century
Week 15	Final Projects	Presentations

Source: Sydney Maresca, 2022

Table 1.2 History of Style 2, Syllabus Calendar

History of Style 2		
Duration	Learning Modules	Activities – In Class
Week 1	Introduction	Syllabus and Learning Goals Building Sources: French Research
Week 2	French Courts 1700 → 1650	Visual Literacy: 17th-Century France Building Sources: Dutch Research
Week 3	Dutch Prosperity 1650 → 1615	Visual Literacy: 17th-Century Netherlands Building Sources: English Research
Week 4	Tudor England 1615 → 1500	Visual Literacy: 16th-Century England Building Sources: Italian Research
Week 5	Italian Renaissance 1600 → 1400	Visual Literacy: Renaissance Italy Building Sources: Medieval Research

(Continued)

Table 1.2 Continued

\<History of Style 2\>		
Duration	**Learning Modules**	**Activities – In Class**
Week 6	Middle Ages 1400 → 1100	Visual Literacy: Medieval Europe Building Sources: Ancient Mediterranean Research
Week 7	Ancient Mediterranean	Visual Literacy: Ancient Mediterranean Building Sources: African and Middle Eastern Research
Week 8	Africa and Middle East	Visual Literacy: Africa & Middle East Building Sources: East Asian Research
Week 9	East Asia	Visual Literacy: East Asia Building Sources: South Asian Research
Week 10	South Asia	Visual Literacy: South Asia Building Sources: Oceania Research
Week 11	Pacific Islands/ Oceania	Visual Literacy: Oceania Building Sources: South and Central American Research
Week 12	South and Central America	Visual Literacy: South and Central America Building Sources: North American Research
Week 13	Individual Meetings	Individual Meetings to Discuss Projects
Week 14	North America	Visual Literacy: North America
Week 15	Final Projects	Presentations

Source: Sydney Maresca, 2022

> I use an arrow when writing time periods, instead of a dash (1950 → 1930). Because I am framing time in a backwards progression, I find that I need a way to differentiate it visually. If I use a dash between the two time periods (1950–1930), people's eyes tend to skip over the numbers and assume that they are written in the traditional chronological format. When writing dates in this course, it is important to convey that we are using time in a different kind of way.

I teach the History of Style at Montclair State University, a two-semester class that covers clothing, architecture, and objects (i.e., research for costumes, sets, and props) from present day to the prehistoric period. The class is taught entirely online in synchronous sessions over Zoom, primarily for students studying theatre design and technology. Previously, I taught a two-semester class at New York University, Period Styles, covering the history of clothing and dress over the same span of time. The class at NYU was taught in person and relied heavily on student interaction with historic and reproduction garments. I re-designed the course while I was teaching at NYU, making two radical changes: I structured the course in reverse-chronological order, and I focused our classwork on objects and object analysis, grounded in Jules Prown's material culture framework.[1] I made a third major change when I began teaching at MSU in an all-online format: I refocused the learning around building visual literacy and research skills, particularly digital research skills. Upending my approach to the teaching and structure of these courses has revealed opportunities to refocus the work around skill building and goals for student learning and success.

The first time I taught a fashion history course, I taught it the way it was presented to me when I was a student: We started at the beginning of time and worked our way forward until the professor got to about 1980 and then ran out of time. In planning my first semester of the class, I leaned on what I knew. I had taken fashion history at least three times, and the classes were all presented in the same historical, chronological order. My professors showed me hundreds of images of people in historical dress in their extensive slideshow lectures week after week, and I filled notebooks with the important historical fashion vocabulary that they presented. It worked for me. I "know" fashion history now and at least some of those important words that I wrote down. Teaching my first fashion history class, I did it the way my teachers taught me. I was surprised when I ran into some major issues.

Teaching fashion history to theatre design students, I built our weekly homework assignments around finding research images – paralleling the kind of research work they would be doing in their design classes. Their weekly assignment was to turn in three research images from the period we would be discussing in class. By starting the course, and therefore the research image assignment, at the beginning of time, I was setting these novice research-image finders a nearly impossible task as their first experience: Finding images from some of the earliest documented periods of human history – the hardest periods for them to research. Prehistoric clothing looks nothing like what a contemporary twenty-year-old understands as clothing. Many students found themselves at a loss, not knowing where to look for research images or how to understand the images they saw when they found them. If I was seeking to build image research skills, this was a poor way to scaffold the assignment – starting with the hardest assignment and working up to the easier work – and I found that my students were struggling to understand what constituted a quality, primary-source research image when they were looking through photos of ancient loom weights and cartoons of cavemen.

In choosing to restructure my course to operate in reverse-chronological order, I wanted to address a number of needs that were not being met by the earlier version of the course. To address the need for expanding the canon of fashion history beyond the traditional narrative of Western civilization, I needed to narrow the scope of what I was trying to accomplish while broadening the source material. I needed to give students twenty-first-century research skills so that they had the confidence to find research that moved beyond the first page of Google image search, including a range of digital, hard-copy, and object-based resources. I needed to scaffold the acquisition of skills so that the course could lean into what the students were already good at as a foundation for building new skills. I needed to build bridges and legibility between the research work we were doing in the theatre department and work that was happening in other fields. And, when taking on the version of the course that includes the history of architecture and décor in addition to the history of clothing, I needed to expand my positioning of what we mean by *style*. Rather than presenting students with a parade of styles to help them memorize periods, I sought to build visual literacy and research skills, giving students the tools to find, read, and interrogate an image as a way of understanding period style.

Building Research Skills

Students immersed in the nonstop visual culture of contemporary social media have a complex visual literacy and an ability to digest and process images that is unparalleled. Consuming digital images is one of their native languages, though there remains room for building depth of analysis and understanding. By structuring this course in reverse-chronological order, the course is able to use the skills that students bring with them – finding images of people and things on their phones and computers – as a foundation for deeper, historically grounded research work. In History of Style, we build research skills through practice. Each week, students must source and turn in nine images from the period we are studying (three images of people in clothes, three images of objects, and three images of buildings). We begin researching in the period in which students are most fluent – today – and build a toolbox of research skills scaffolded onto their foundation of contemporary digital media consumption. These weekly research images become the framework for the week's class discussion. I compile the images into a slide show; organize the images to draw out themes, raise questions, and help build connections; and lead the students in a group conversation built around investigating the style of the period through their research images.

Sample Assignment

Weekly Homework: Research Images

Research images are due by 9:00 a.m. the Thursday before class. Cite your sources!

Nine research images from [PERIOD/PLACE]

At least six of the images must be from [SOURCE, e.g., magazines] and must include:

- three buildings
- three objects
- three people wearing clothes (head-to-toe images)

Image Titles

Each image must be labeled with a title that contains:

- The name of what is pictured in the image (e.g., halogen lamp, Cesar Chavez wearing plaid shirt and trousers, the Eiffel Tower, etc.)
- The place the object was made
- The cultural affiliation of the object, if known
- The date the object was made

Citations

All images must be cited as follows, using the *Chicago Manual of Style* format (https://cmosshoptalk.com/2016/03/15/how-do-i-cite-an-image/)

Sourcing the images can be easy for the students at first. The assignment for the first period we cover, contemporary, is to take their own pictures of people and objects from around their world, giving us a richly detailed research portrait of this specific place and time: In our case, Montclair, New Jersey, right now. (See Figure 1.2) The only research tools students need to bring to the assignment are a digital camera and an eye for details, which I feel confident that they already possess. The second week's assignment is to find images from the last three years. Those images can be sourced from

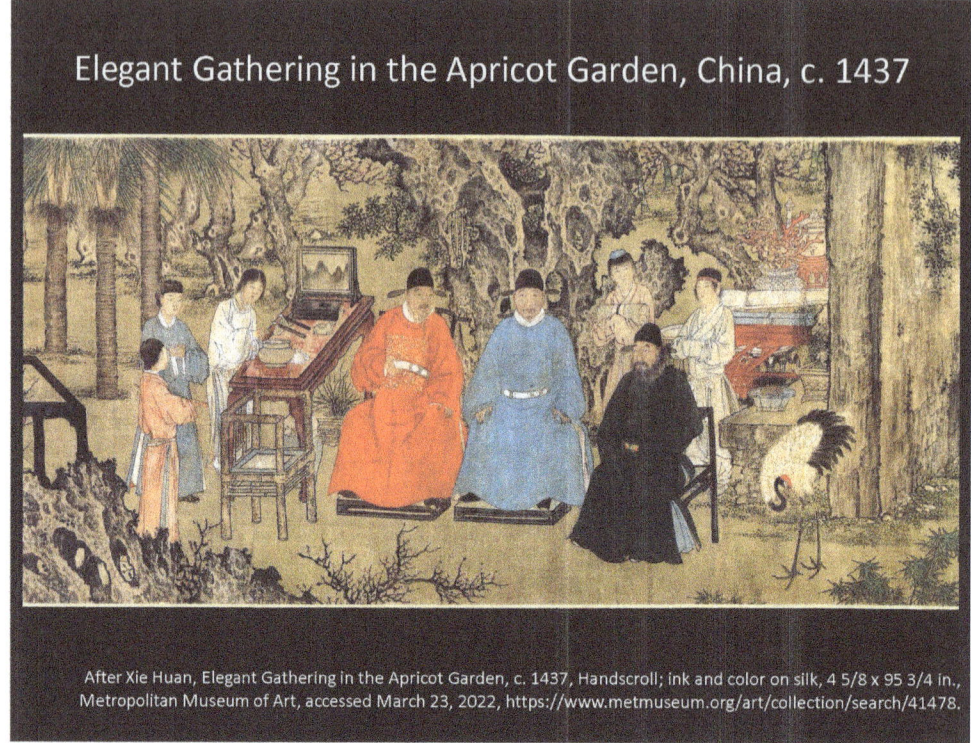

Figure 1.1 Student's weekly homework research image with title and citation: "Elegant Gathering in the Apricot Garden," 1437

anywhere on the internet, including the social media and internet image searches the students are already swimming in. However, in order to turn those memes and Snapchats into quality research, students must include a complete citation with each of their images, using a recognized scholarly citation format.[2] Beginning with research sources most students are already confident with allows me to focus early assignment feedback on technical details like citations and analysis. (See Figure 1.1.)

I place a strong emphasis on citations for images in our classwork. In my own design education, I learned to be a greedy researcher, grabbing images from anywhere that inspired me, neither crediting the image makers nor leaving a trail of breadcrumbs for future researchers or designers who might want to know more about the image and where it came from. Neglecting to include complete citations with research images denies the image makers the credit for their work, removes valuable context for understanding meaning and information conveyed in the image, and renders the image potentially untraceable for future researchers. After two decades of costume design, my greedy research has left me with binders full of incredible images and no

Figure 1.2 Contemporary dress, Montclair, NJ
Source: Photo by Michael Brinskele, 2022

information about what they are or where they came from. Taking the time to include complete citations with image- and object-based research elevates both individual theatre designers' work and the field as a whole by using formatting that is recognized across disciplines while at the same time making it citable by other scholars. I tell my students that their citations are gifts to future researchers and to themselves, providing detailed information that enables interested researchers to track down those images again.

In order to help students build a broader range of research sources, each week, I take time in class to introduce a type of resource – magazines, newspapers, museums, online archives. I require that their next week's research include images from that new resource; for example: The week we are studying the mid-nineteenth century, students are required to use museums' digital collections to source their images. Rather than tell my students what not to do ("Don't just use Google image search!"), I offer them productive replacements for a research tool that, while it has its uses, should not be their only resource.

Figure 1.3 *Describe this object. Start with the big picture and then move on to details. Describe only what you can see.* Unknown Chimú maker; feathered shirt; Peru, 13th–15th century; cotton, feathers, silver; H. 10 in. x W. 18 in.

Source: Metropolitan Museum of Art

Building Visual Literacy

Students are confident that they can see what is in an image, but can they read it? *Visual literacy* is used to describe reading and understanding the messages conveyed by visual media.[3] Students who are trying to build reading literacy practice by reading texts. In this course, we build visual literacy by reading images – by both digesting a high volume of images (weekly research assignments) and diving into deeper analysis of individual images. The students' research images become the foundation for our in-class discussions. Each week, I compile all the students' images (well over 100) into a slideshow for class. In building the slide shows, I try to create opportunities for discoveries and connection making. I prompt students to look for meanings in the images and to question what kind of biases might be present, what the perspective of the image maker might be, and what the perspective of the person or object represented in the image might be.

Turning 117 student research images into a slide presentation for class each week is a lot of work. It means I will never get to the point in teaching the class when I can just cruise and rely on the old and excellent slide shows I have already built. But, knowing myself and how I teach, it means that I will continue to be totally present for my students and that I will be actively building questions and content for every class. I will never have the opportunity to get bored and grumpy about teaching the same thing year after year because a new group of students means a new set of materials each year. If a student feels disappointed that a particular topic isn't being addressed in the class, they have the opportunity to submit images that can direct the conversations to that topic. With practice, I have built efficiencies into the slide presentation–making process, and I know to schedule two to three hours each week to prepare. I will confess that I have some ringer images up my sleeve. If the students have overlooked something really crucial or if I get 93 images of Marie Antionette's left shoe, I am very willing to sneak some extra objects and images into the conversation.

In addition to keeping me actively connected to the work in the class, it is guaranteed that the students have a personal connection to at least some of the material because nine of the images/objects were ones that they have found themselves for class that day. (Three objects, three buildings, and three images of clothed people.) It has been a fascinating way to make room for diversity in the course because the discussion is driven by the students' background and interests. There is no way I would have been able to source some of the images and objects that my students have shared in their research homework: Images from growing up in Korea or on an army base in Vietnam or from old family pictures of life in mid-century Finland. The classes are richer for their contributions. By the time we get through a class session, the students have had the opportunity to think through over 100 images representing objects, spaces, and people in clothes from a specific period. Through our work in class, using research sourced by the students, we build a visual literacy for the style of the period: The lines, shapes, colors, materials, and forms that tend to reflect the cultural expression of a particular place and moment in human history.

Building Object-Based Histories

In this course, we are not looking at images for their own sake but because the images contain representations of objects that reflect period, place, and style. I use an object-based, material-culture approach to thinking through the history of style. This means that we spend time in class looking closely at specific objects (or images of objects) and exploring what we can learn from the objects themselves. In striving for a more inclusive history of style, productive researchers can learn to look beyond the texts in libraries and the paintings in museums. Throughout history, many voices have been excluded from the written archive, and it is possible to help recover the stories of some of those who may have been left out of the text-based records through the study and understanding of the objects that people designed, made, desired, bought, sold, used, repaired, discarded, or saved.

There are a number of parallels between the work of material culture scholarship and the work of a theatre designer. Both use objects as carriers of history and meaning to help tell stories about people and cultures. In using this recognized, scholarly methodology, the observation and analysis of historic objects we do in class have the potential to make our work translatable across fields, connecting our theatre thinking to history, art history, anthropology, sociology, archaeology, and the sciences. We observe, analyze, and speculate about objects in class through both individual and group projects that invite deeper thinking about the things that are in the world. This is not only research for design; this is history. Even though the process, as proposed by Prown, is the kind of work we have been doing as theatre artists for generations, grounding the work in a foundation of material culture scholarship has the potential to position theatre makers as part of the larger history-making conversation.

Re-Fashioning Time

The first time I taught time backwards was a little rocky – it took a long time to reprogram my own brain, and there were some things about the way I did it that were confusing for some of my students. I was bad at remembering that we were dealing with time backwards. Because the rest of our world is oriented to think about time going in the forward direction, I learned that I had to be rigorously consistent about how I was referring to time in the class, or I would cause confusion. Three years after I started teaching fashion history in reverse-chronological order, I looked at my bookshelf and realized all my costume books were still organized in the traditional forward movement of time – no wonder it was hard for me to be consistent in the way I was talking about time. I re-organized my books. With practice and consistency, I have built a way of dealing with time in this course that feels both accessible and productive as a tool for understanding cultural expressions of style.

Framing things by time is a relatively efficient method for divvying up subjects in the globalized modern and early modern worlds, and it works relatively neatly going as far back as the Industrial Revolution. In a world with global communication networks, organizing by time can make room for global conversations. For me, the organization seemed to break down when I wanted to narrow in on older periods – the bias towards the evolutionary, myth-building narrative of Western civilization starts to show through the cracks as the system falls apart. If we're talking about the Middle Ages, we're really talking about the Middle Ages in Europe. Ignoring that "Middle Ages" is a geographically specific description allows us to ignore the hundreds (thousands?) of other cultures that were active at the same time. For example, Cahokia, in what is now Southern Illinois, was thriving and in 1250 had a population that was larger than London's.[4] Is that part of what we mean when we teach the Middle Ages? Is there any kind of relationship between a pair of poulaines and pair of copper ear spools?

In the course's first semester, students are free to submit research images from any geographical region, as long as the images are from the right period. In approaching the second semester, covering 1700 → prehistory, it became necessary to be very clear not only about time but also about location. When we got as far as the beginning of the Industrial Revolution and the early days of global trade, I exploded the timeline and divided subjects up by geographies, shining a light on our earlier bias towards American and Eurocentric expressions of style. Considering time in conversation with geography – period and place – allows us to address cultures, colonialisms, and materiality. Objects are directly connected to the land. They are made for use in response to the regional environment from locally sourced plants, animals, and minerals. Trade relationships may expand the pool of available resources, but even imported materials are local to somewhere. Using those materials to create objects that convey style speaks to specific trade relationships and knowledge networks, contributing to personal or community expressions of identity and status. When we are looking at the history of style, we are looking at the history of people through the objects they made and used to express a particular understanding of self across a span of individual moments in time and space. In History of Style, I aim to build students' research skills, visual literacy, and object-based analysis tools. We build these skills through practice, both as a group in class and individually through research projects. Building these skills not only helps students tell richer, more well-informed stories in their theatre practice but also offers them the opportunity to use the history of dress, architecture, and décor as a framework to interrogate world history.

Bikini – Research, Analysis, Synthesis

In this exercise, students read selections from a scholarly article in small teams, answer questions in response to the article, and build image-based research in support of the ideas in their responses. However, I don't use the word *read* when talking about what we are going to do with the article

> because we are not going to sit down and read the whole article. I use words like *tackle* and *dissect* because students are going to work together and use the article to find the writer's ideas in order to explore and discuss them. Rather than ask the students to take on this reading as homework, we dissect the reading in class. Students tackle a complex and challenging academic article about a historic object. They take on the text through team reading, group discussions, and synthesis through image research.

Teresia Teaiwa's 1994 article "Bikinis and Other s/Pacific n/Oceans" offers a challenging cultural history of why the two-piece bathing suit shares a name with an atoll in the Marshall Islands.[5] Students read selections from the article in small groups and work as a team to create responses to Teaiwa's ideas through image research. Student teams create three slides in response to their reading and discussions. Slide one asks students to reflect on their personal relationship with the material. Teaiwa poses the question to readers "What does the word *bikini* evoke for you?" Students create a slide in response to Teaiwa's question, generating their own writing and sourcing images that support their ideas. Of course, they are required to include complete citations for all their images. Slide two asks students to identify the problems proposed in the article and to find one or two images that support their answer. Students are asked to tackle Teaiwa's multi-layered history of colonialism and gender expression and to convey their understanding through found images. Slide three asks students to think through the reading from a fashion history perspective. Students are asked to pull out the names of the fashion historians Teaiwa cites in her work, situating the conversation about clothing as part of a continuing scholarly topic. Through both writing and image research, students are then asked to note connections or disconnections between contemporary conceptualizations of the bikini and the "traditional" clothing of the Bikini islands. Additionally, students are asked to reflect on how contemporary conceptualizations of the bikini relate to European-American clothing in the mid-twentieth century. Then we come back together as a class to listen to and discuss the conversations and ideas that came out of each group's work.

Building and discussing research image responses to a text parallels the research work that is done in design for performance. Like a designer, students read a text, build a personal relationship to the text through their understanding of their own experience, expand out to a broader understanding of someone else's experience as described in the text, and develop image research to illuminate their ideas and help express those ideas to others. Coming back

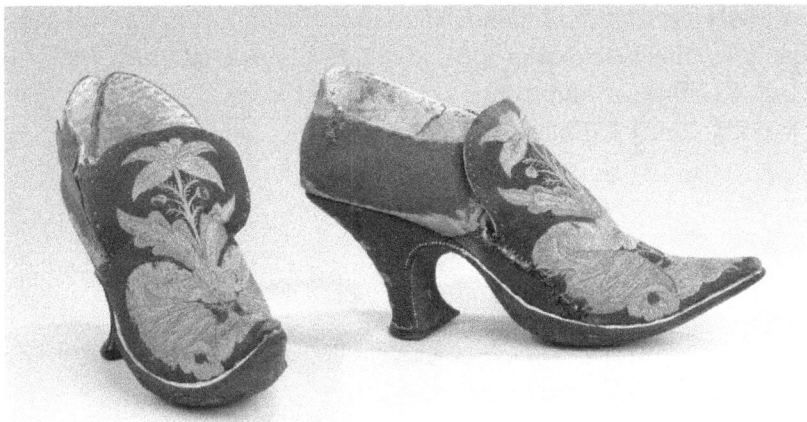

Figure 1.4 *Imagine what it would be like to use or interact with this object. Imagine touching, feeling, hearing, smelling, using, wearing, repairing, and/or making this object.* Unknown European maker; shoes; Europe, 1690–1710; leather and silk

Source: Metropolitan Museum of Art

together to discuss the ideas they've developed as a group mirrors the openness and confidence that a designer must bring with them to a design meeting, sharing their research with the team and using responses to the research to refine their ideas and ways in which the ideas might be expressed.

Through this exercise, students are able to make connections between their own personal experiences around body and identity and some of the deeply layered and complicated experiences of identity, colonialism, constructs of gender and race, cultural eradication, and environmental destruction and the cultural, global, and personal impacts of the United States military's actions that are embedded in a word that might have seemed like it was simply describing a swimsuit. In addition, students build critical-thinking confidence, knowing that they have tackled some of the major concepts discussed in a dense, scholarly text.

Notes

1 Prown, Jules David. "Mind in Matter: An Introduction to Material Culture Theory and Method." *Winterthur Portfolio* 17, no. 1, April 1, 1982, 1–19.
2 "How Do I Cite an Image?" In *CMOS Shop Talk from The Chicago Manual of Style*, https://cmosshoptalk.com/2016/03/15/how-do-i-cite-an-image/
3 *Visual Literacy Today*, https://visualliteracytoday.org/. The International Visual Literacy Association, https://ivla.org/

4 National Park Service. *Cahokia Mounds State Historic Site & Interpretive Center*, www.nps.gov/places/cahokia-mounds-state-historic-site.htm
5 Teaiwa, Teresia K. "Bikinis and Other s/Pacific n/Oceans." *The Contemporary Pacific* 6, no. 1, April 1, 1994, 87–109.

2

Research Methods for Fashion History and Technology

Grace Cochran Keenan

Course Description

The two main goals of this course are to develop a working vocabulary and to learn how to research. I help the students develop these skills by presenting a global overview of clothing and society in various times and places. In general, I cover the six inhabited continents, but I focus in on specific countries and regions to direct the lecture while also making it known to the students that this is a small piece of the larger world at any given time. For example, when covering North American Indian tribes, I show a map that lists the regions inhabited by the various Native American tribes, but we focus on the Algonquins.

At the end of this course, the students know the general style lines found across time periods and regions that are covered in this course as well as having a working knowledge of various vocabulary words commonly used to discuss clothing. In addition, they know how and where to look for credible sources when researching any given period or region.

> School: Kent State University
> Department: School of Theatre and Dance
> Student Level/Description: Upper Undergraduate Design Elective/Graduate-Level Program Requirement Course

> Class Size: 15–25
>
> Hours/Week: 75 minutes, twice a week
>
> Class Format: Synchronous in person (Though the first time it was asynchronous online)
>
> Text or Core Materials:
>
> Edwards, Lydia. *How to Read A Dress: A Guide to Changing Fashions from the 16th to the 20th Century*, Bloomsbury, 2017.
>
> Edwards, Lydia. *How to Read A Suit: A Guide to Changing Fashions from the 16th to the 20th Century*, Bloomsbury, 2020.
>
> Welters, Linda and Lillethun, Abby. *Fashion History, A Global View*, Bloomsbury, 2018.
>
> Other materials reserved through university library
>
> Types of Access Needed: Internet, access to Adobe Sparks

Change Can be Slow . . . or Very, Very Fast

I first took a clothing history course in graduate school and was given the opportunity to teach the course my last semester. I delivered the course as it was delivered to me, in a traditional "Western European silhouettes from 1700 to 1980" sort of way. When I began teaching at Kent State University as an adjunct, I was asked what courses I might be able to develop for their curriculum that would fill some gaps. I developed and presented a costume history course in 2015 based on the course I had both taken and taught in graduate school.

Over the next three to four years, I slowly tinkered with the course, updating images and trying to expand beyond what I had originally developed to move beyond a white, Eurocentric approach, finding more BIPOC images (especially before 1850) in Western silhouettes. This was good and necessary work but did not directly address my and my students' dissatisfaction with the course's limited view of the history of clothing.

I had always thought that changing this course as much as I did would be a slow process over multiple semesters. Then came the COVID-19 pandemic. The pandemic brought a reduction in my role as it pertained to production work as there is little need for a draper or tailor in a virtual theatrical production. This created space for me to directly address my desire to completely start over with my course and create one that covered clothing history through a more global lens. I threw out my old syllabus and started over.

A Research Perspective

When developing a more global clothing course, it is necessary to pick a lens and approach that best fit the learning objectives that a particular course needs to meet. For this course, I needed to go back to the reason we needed a costume history course in the curriculum.

I knew that change was needed, but I do not think I had the words for why; over time, I realized that the real value in the course is in learning how to research clothing so that when one must do so for the specific time and place in which a production is set, they have the tools to do it. I don't need to "make sure I cover" anything in particular, and this approach does not put pressure on me to cover absolutely everything in the history of clothing. It actually creates mental space to think beyond how I was taught and have taught clothing history to create a course that does not uphold a Eurocentric narrative with which I do not agree.

Instead, I focused on how one does research for a specific time and place. This mimics what we do with production and allows me to jump around the globe to focus on a variety of places, silhouettes, and clothing vocabularies.

> **Chosen Evolution**
>
> This can seem like an overwhelming task. Sometimes just cutting down one lecture to make room for something new can be a way to start. I still find places I can do that in the current set-up of the course. My intention is to continue to make more room to look at other cultures and areas around the globe.

Course Objectives
- Recognize general style lines found in periods and regions covered in the course;
- Have a working knowledge of common vocabulary when discussing clothing for a theatrical production;
- Know how and where to look for research sources when approaching any given period and region for a theatrical production; and
- Graduate students: Be able to look at extant garments and describe their various attributes.

Learning Outcomes

- Students will be able to utilize a variety of reliable sources for primary research;
- Students will be able to look at resource images and describe what they observe utilizing proper vocabulary;
- Students will know how to write proper citations for various sources of research;
- Students will be able to present and discuss their research in a way that can be understood by those who may not be familiar with a particular region and time;
- Students will have a personal list of reliable resources to go to for primary resource images;
- Students will be able to recognize the general style lines of the various regions and periods we cover; and
- Students will have a working vocabulary to discuss clothing from various periods and regions.

Table 2.1 Syllabus Calendar

Week	Class Topic One	Class Topic Two
1	Toolbox Day Syllabus Adobe Sparks How to conduct research How to cite research	Fashion History Theory What is costume history? What is fashion history? Why do we study it? What are the limitations of the way it has been studied in the past? What is the purpose of this course?
2	16th Century 1500–1599 (Tudor Clothing)	North America (East Woodland Tribes)
3	17th Century 1600–1699 (Stuart/Louis XIV)	Mesoamerica – Aztecs
4	South America – Andes Region	18th Century Europe 1700–1789
5	Europe 1790–1829	Europe 1790–1829
6	Europe/United States 1830–1869	Enslaved Persons' Clothing
7	Europe/United States 1870–1899	Mourning Culture Across the Globe

Week	Class Topic One	Class Topic Two
8	Asia: China Before 1900	Asia: Korea Before 1900
9	Asia: Japan Before 1900	Asia: India Before 1900
10	Europe 1900–1929	Library Day
11	Spring Break: No Class	Spring Break: No Class
12	Europe: 1930–1959	Final Project Peer Review Day/ Work Day Library Day
13	Polynesian: Hawaii	Europe 1947–1969
14	Sub-Saharan Africa Before 1900	Europe: 1970–1989
15	Wrap Up How has your perspective on the study of clothing history changed? Is there a particular area we studied that you felt drawn to? Check in on Final Project	Work Day/Library Day Sometimes I cancel class and offer to meet individually with students
16	Final Project Presentations	

Source: Grace Cochran Keenan, 2021

Since my original course covered European clothing, my first step was to reduce the amount of European clothing I covered. I made some deep cuts and major changes to my lectures and how in depth I discussed European clothing.

I started this work in May of 2020, in conjunction with the ReDressing the Narrative virtual conference run by Chloe Chapin and Christianne Myers. I did an initial revamp of the course on paper during the conference, just to try and visualize what I wanted to see if I could fit it all into one semester. It was good to start with some kind of framework; I had my course objectives but little in the way of how to actually make it work. I had also figured out during this time that I would use *Fashion History: A Global View* by Linda Welters and Abby Lillethun as a required text.

During the fall of 2020, I met with the director of Kent State University's Center for Teaching and Learning, Dr. Jennifer Marcinkiewicz, and Edith

Serkownek, head of the Kent State Fashion Library, to discuss various aspects of the course as I worked through its restructuring. With Dr. Marcinkiewicz, I explained how I had taught the course in the past, what my learning outcomes were, and how I wanted to restructure the course. By the time I met with Dr. Marcinkiewicz, I had already gotten my course calendar closer to what the final version would be for the spring of 2021. I expressed that I was looking for different projects and ways to engage the students in the learning that would be fun and active as my previous projects for the course no longer worked with my updated learning objectives. Among her recommendations were various digital platforms that could be used to support the students' learning. The last one she mentioned was Adobe Sparks, a platform where students could create posters or fact sheets for each time period. This program eventually led to the research presentation projects, the primary weekly project in the course.

Dr. Marcinkiewicz also recommended strategies like reaching out to the library to help me cultivate articles and materials for the students. Meeting with Professor Edith Serkownek, the head librarian for Kent State's Fashion Library, was on my list, but this encouraged me to meet with her sooner rather than later. When Professor Serkownek and I met, I was most interested in what readings and articles might be good alternatives to the most common, Eurocentric texts many of us are familiar with. Professor Serkownek pointed out some resources in the library's database that she thought would be helpful, as well as mentioning two books, *How to Read a Dress* and *How to Read a Suit*, both by Lydia Edwards. I already owned these books but had not considered them as they are not traditional textbooks; after reviewing the texts through the lens of this course, I added these as required texts as well. Their layout and explanations of the images was similar to how I wanted my students to interpret their research for the research project presentations. There were many other readings and articles for the various regions and time periods we covered; those were all on reserve for the students through our university's library.

Once I was able to find readings, I started fleshing out the syllabus with the readings that I wanted to include. With the three required texts as the main sources, I started plugging in other articles I found. Kassia St. Clair's book *The Golden Thread* was particularly helpful as it is full of chapters that cover clothing around the globe from various time periods and, additionally, is more readable than an academic article. I also added certain YouTube videos to the readings to help the students see how the layers of clothing worked together for particular periods and/or regions. An important aspect of designing and making historical clothing is knowing what layers are necessary to create the desired shapes. Otherwise, how can you make a piece list or know what needs to be prepped and fit before draping can begin? The

"Getting Dressed" series by CrowsEyeProduction and the BBC show *A Stitch in Time* were both useful for European silhouettes. I utilized some YouTube videos to cover historical context for some of the modules as well. This mix of film, articles, and chapters led to the students doing more of the required reading than I had ever seen in previous iterations of this course. Many of the students, as part of their discussion board posts the first semester, commented on what reading was their favorite or how something had encouraged them to seek out other resources, which is what I had hoped the readings would do. The readings and videos were all very consumable for the students with only a few being more "academic" writing. This suited the population I am teaching particularly well. This was not a class for an academic researcher but for a practice-based researcher. The material I exposed them to needed to reflect that goal.

The first semester that I offered the new version of this course, it was an online and asynchronous course since we were still in the throes of the COVID-19 pandemic. I spent my time developing and recording my lectures and making the course workable and accessible in an online environment. This was neither a benefit nor a hinderance; it was just how it worked. I think reworking this course in terms of weeks as opposed to individual lecture days was an effective way to wrap my brain around the course changes.

The second semester I taught this course, I was back in the classroom. I presented the course as a typical lecture course like I had taught in my previous iteration. Offering it for the first time in front of the students, I wanted to present it in a method I was comfortable with to be sure the material worked. This was illuminating in terms of more readily seeing things I wanted to continue to change and improve on with the students' direct reactions.

Student Favorite

One of the students' favorite projects has been our final project. This project allows them to do a deep dive into any region/time period they want. The purpose is to be as specific as possible (for example, Madagascar from 1900 through 1910). This mimics researching a production, when you focus on a specific place and time and work on it throughout the second half of the semester. They are charged with creating a PowerPoint presentation of their research that should be set up like a mini lecture (similar to what they see in my lectures). There are multiple check points and library days devoted to this project, as seen in the calendar. The students love being able to focus on an area and time period they are interested in, and much of the time, I get to learn something new from the students.

Table 2.2 Research Presentation Rubric (Weekly Homework)

Features	Points	Comments
Five Primary Resource Images	25 pts	• Must be primary resource images from the time and place we are covering in class. Can be paintings of the clothing of the era, extant pieces, photographs (once we are far enough in history), etc.
Five Summaries of Fashion Elements in Each Image	25 pts	• A four-to-five-sentence summary of fashion elements for each resource image • Must be written in student's own voice • Must utilize vocabulary covered in class/ found in their research to describe the fashion elements observed in the image
Five Citations for Each Primary Resource Image	25 pts	• Citations are done in MLA format • Each image is from a different resource

Source: Grace Cochran Keenan, 2021

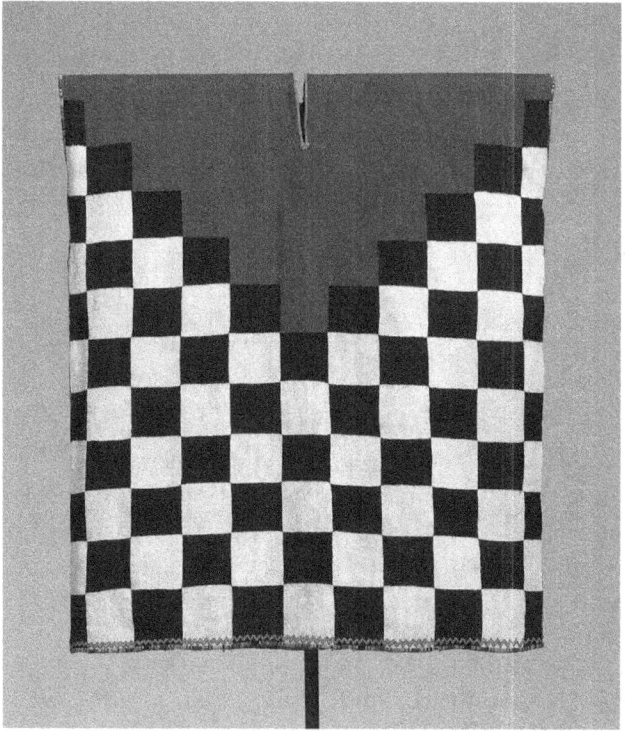

Figure 2.1 Example of research presentation project: Checkerboard Tunic: tapestry-woven tunic; Inca; 16th Century. The emphasis of this project is noting and describing details, proper citation, and image contextualization

Source: Elaine Bodenberg, Kent State University, costume minor

The student's text included with the image is as follows:

Student's Description: This tunic is from the Incan Empire in the 16th century, likely after Spanish contact in the region. It is made from camelid fiber, a popular textile due to the abundance of alpacas, llama, and vicunas. The tunic in this style was popular for men and usually called the uncu, which was stitched at the sides. This checkerboard print reminds me of the tocapu geometric prints, which were mostly reserved for the upper class/nobility. Andean weaving techniques like this were very important to the Incas and got very complex for some designs.
Student's Citation: Designer unknown. Checkerboard Tunic. Camelid Fiber. Argentina, Peru, or Bolivia. 16th Century. Metropolitan Museum of Art, New York. www.metmuseum.org/art/collection/search/751901?&exhibitionId=%7b3b5ff8a3-a6fd-99f7-8395014924be%7d&old=751901&pkglds=473&pg=0&rpp=20&pos=83&ft=*&offset=20.

Curricular Connections

This course is a design elective for our BFA design and technology students, a theatre elective for our BA theatre studies students, and a major elective for our MFA design and technology students.

I place a heavy emphasis on the fact that we are not just learning about the clothing of a specific time and place; we are also practicing the skills that are required over and over when putting on a production: Conducting research on the time and setting of a production in order to guide our design and construction choices. We just happen to be doing it through the lens of clothing across the globe. I also, from my background as a draper and tailor, discuss the pattern shapes of various silhouettes as they existed in the times and places they were created, as well as how some silhouettes can be recreated for the stage with contemporary materials and with the movement needs of a contemporary performer in mind.

When I think about what it has changed beyond my classroom, this was one of, if not the first of, the courses that went through a heavy de-centering of European history in my department. By sharing what I have been working on with my colleagues both at my university and at other institutions, I hope I have been able to show one version of how to practically apply the idea of a global clothing course.

It certainly has changed how my students respond to the material and what they view as available resources for their own research. For example, as part of their research for the final project, a student reached out to the Ukrainian Museum archives to see pieces in person. This led to a job offer for the summer working in the archives and an opportunity to put together an exhibit for the museum. This allowed my students to see other avenues of employment available to them as well as why it can be so beneficial to do research beyond what they find on the internet.

> **Committee Checks!**
> When updating your course, check with your curriculum committee about whether the catalogue description or the catalogue number needs to be changed. When I updated the course description, I was told that I had changed the course so much that a new number needed to be assigned to the course. Lean on your curriculum committee to help navigate this! I came up against a lot of bureaucracy that the curriculum committee chair was able to help me navigate.

Conclusion

I am very excited with how this course has turned out so far. Overall, the students were able to see a huge breadth of clothing history, and they were so much more engaged with the material than I had seen in previous semesters. This way of teaching the course also allowed students to research things that were more specific to their interests. While working on the research presentation projects for Europe, pre-1700, one student expressed interest in the Moors in Italy and Spain. Their research included lots of imagery of Afro-Europeans from these regions, which was great for other students to see and provided room for the student to share their knowledge in that realm. Restructuring this course was a huge lift, and I often felt like I was building the tracks in front of the train that first semester. I am grateful that the pandemic gave me this space as I don't know how I could have redesigned this course as extensively as I did without spreading the work across many semesters.

One of the main things I would still like to change is the section on European clothing history. Right now, it still comprises a large proportion of the material covered in the course. This became especially apparent the second semester I taught this class after redesigning it. There is much in my European lectures that could still be cut or redone so I have more room for other regions. I'd like to add at least one or two more lectures on other Native American tribes. I would also like to add more regions from the African continent to the course – right now, I discuss the Kuba Kingdom as a single lecture and Uganda when discussing mourning around the world. I'd like to perhaps look at regions in the northern part of the continent. I think continuing that work is important. The course is better than it was, but there is still much to do. I also think about changing the structure of the course so we focus on Europe for so many weeks, then Asia for so many weeks, then South America, etc. This would also help de-center the European lectures.

In addition, my Western European lectures currently focus on Britain, France, and the United States. This was the default when first redoing the course as I had those lecture materials ready, and the other areas needed a much bigger lift on my part. I need to edit and shift focus so I can look at other countries and regions to include more from Italy, Spain, Greece, Russia, Germany, and others.

The final thing I want to work on is utilizing flipped learning in this course. It is a pedagogical approach in which students learn information outside the classroom and then practically apply that information inside the classroom. Its focus is increasing and capitalizing on active learning in the classroom and leaving passive learning activities for their homework. I already utilize flipped learning in all my construction and pattern-making courses – the students watch videos of me doing the work outside the classroom, and then class time is their primary work time. When I taught costume history in person, I delivered it as a typical lecture, and that is just not as exciting, nor does it enable various learning modalities. I think my students were more engaged with the materials and the literature when I taught this course as an asynchronous online course than when we were in person. At the very least, more of the students were both reading the texts and listening to my lectures. I do not believe the students were reading the articles I assigned when I taught this in person.

I believe the key to this is my role as a maker. As a maker, I spend much of my time thinking about how to create the items we are looking at or how the items would have been created in the time and place they originate from. For example, I'm interested in getting back-strap looms when discussing both the Aztecs and the Incas so the students understand in a more tactile way what I mean when discussing the high monetary value of cloth in a time when it had to be made by hand. This would also allow me to bring into the classroom my love of certain crafts that I don't get to teach on a regular basis, like tatting and embroidery. I think this will be the key to getting the students more excited and engaged with the material. The making will serve as a reminder that these items we are studying are not just words and pictures on a page but real, three-dimensional items that people took the time to make: A conscious choice people of the past made in how they wished to express themselves to the world and their communities.

3

Conscious Fashion History

Camille Benda

School: California Institute of the Arts

Department: School of Theatre/School of Critical Studies

Student Level/Description: BFA 3, BFA 4, MFA levels, counts for critical studies credits, most are emphases in costume design, critical studies, and/or fashion history

Class Size: 25 maximum

Format: In-person lecture and lab

Text or Core Materials:

Allaire, Christian. *The Power of Style*, Annick Press, 2021.

Miller, Monica L. *Slaves to Fashion: Black Dandyism and the Styling of Black Diasporic Identity*, Duke University Press, 2009.

Welters, Linda and Lillethun, Abby. *Fashion History, A Global View*, Bloomsbury, 2018.

Additional Suggested Reading:

Edwards, Lydia. *How To Read A Dress: A Guide to Changing Fashions from the 16th to the 20th Century*, Bloomsbury, 2017.

Edwards, Lydia. *How To Read A Suit: A Guide to Changing Fashions from the 16th to the 20th Century*, Bloomsbury, 2020.

Eicher, Joanne B. *Dress and Ethnicity*, Berg, 1999.

Eicher, Joanne B., Evenson, Sandra Lee, and Lutz, Hazel A. *The Visible Self: Global Perspectives on Dress, Culture and Society*, Fairchild Publications, 2008.

Hollander, Anne. *Sex and Suits*, Alfred A. Knopf, 1994.

Reilly, Andrew and Barry, Ben, eds. *Crossing Gender Boundaries, Fashion to Create, Disrupt and Transcend*, Intellect Publishing, 2020.

Ribeiro, Aileen and Cumming, Valerie. *The Visual History of Costume*, BT Batsford Ltd., 1997.

Types of Access Needed: Hard-copy books, library, internet, PDF articles

Expanded Practice

This course examines inclusive practices in fashion, costume, and dress history studies, both historical and contemporary. Students look at not only "his" story and "her" story, but "their" story and "our" story through art, photography, painting, sculpture, mixed media, and social media. Waiting around the corner of many famous paintings or photographs are subjects of color, non-Western subjects, and LGBTQIA+ subjects. The class dives into a circular and inclusive way of looking at history and empowers students to become equitable image researchers and interpreters.

Research projects will focus on society and culture of all social classes, rather than on the most famous or wealthiest at the top of the pyramid. Students will learn how to find high-quality fashion and dress images, how to use them in their work, and how theatre designers (with a focus on costume designers) can be advocates for diversity and equity in casting. Students investigate what belonging means, who has the power to include or exclude, and how clothing plays a role in nonverbally and symbolically transmitting crucial clues to who we are as humans and individuals and, as a result, how performance and theatre can be culture-changing art forms.

Fashion, dress, and costume history is an expanded practice exploring the relationship between fashion, the body, literature, art, design theory and human existence. Topics for this class include but are not limited to subcultures, anthropology (global culture and dress), fashion technology, social history, cultural competence, individual fashion designers, costumes in film and theatre, textiles, surface decoration, construction, and manufacturing.

Course Objectives
- Explore an inclusive Western dress history image database focused on Ancient Egypt to the modern day;
- Define and understand inclusive, equitable, and diverse research methods through class discussion and homework assignments;
- Highlight what excluded groups can be re-integrated into an equitable view of fashion history;
- Question the "default" in traditional dress history, gaining an awareness of difference and how fashion history can look outside the canon of typical dress history sources; and
- Develop a comprehensive bibliography of books/periodicals/museum databases on the subject that include diverse sources and investigate classic texts that might need contextualizing or reframing.

BFA Learning Goals specific to the BFA in Critical Studies
- CS Goal 1: Investigate and analyze key events, movements, and ideas in a diverse range of subject areas relevant to course topic, demonstrating comprehension of diverse methodologies with a range of global and cultural contexts and perspectives;
- CS Goal 2: Collect and organize quantitative information related to course material;
- CS Goal 3: Write independently using sustained analytical and evidence-based reasoning and clear communication; and
- CS Goal 4: Research including the employment of library, internet, and database searches to find and evaluate relevant and reliable sources.

Learning Outcomes
By the end of this course, students will be able to:

- Visually recognize the main eras of fashion history through painting, photography, sculpture, engravings, and sketches;
- Engage in deep, meaningful fashion history research. In this context, "meaningful" can be defined as follows: a) Recognize and understand basic dress history terms and apply them to describing a full outfit, b) briefly detail the cultural significance of the outfit, and c) analyze the outfit's relationship to political dynamics, gender equality, and social class;
- Understand the contribution of marginalized and underrepresented groups to fashion history and the political, social, and economic climates these groups existed within and the challenges they faced;

- Develop broad research skills and understand why they are needed;
- Question and contextualize all research sources, from primary source materials to social media to classic dress history texts;
- Form unique opinions about fashion history topics based on their own personal experiences, cultural family history, and individual research passions; and
- Become advocates for diversity, equity, access, and inclusivity in fashion and dress studies by using excellent research and ideation in their creative practices.

Catalyst for Change

The catalyst for Conscious Fashion History was the 2019 Provost's Research and Practice Fellowship at CalArts – a summer fellowship in which a student fellow, Lily Windsor, and I developed core themes around re-centering equity, diversity, and inclusivity in dress history. The overall goal was to develop fresh curriculum for teaching dress and fashion history, with specific sub-goals in mind:

- Create an inclusive Western dress history image database focused on Ancient Egypt to the modern day;
- Identify a fluid framework for documentation that can be expanded and edited;
- Define inclusive, equitable, and diverse research methods;
- Highlight what excluded groups can be re-included;
- Question the "white/Western default" in traditional dress history; and
- Develop a comprehensive bibliography of books/periodicals/museum databases on the subject.

At the end of the 2019 fellowship, we had created a database of publications that reflected innovative ways of looking at dress history, and many of the images found made their way into the slides for Conscious Fashion History. In 2022, I was awarded a second Research and Practice Fellowship, focusing specifically on gender, dress, fashion, and costume. My 2022 student fellow, Ashley Snyder, and I added approximately 160 new entries focusing on dress and gender to the overall resource list started in 2019.

The list is alphabetized and annotated with links to WorldCat and the CalArts library and includes notes and categories of EDI topics. The 2022 fellowship also added approximately 50 articles on dress and gender to the shared Google Drive, which now reside in a folder that will be accessible to all students. Over 300 photos of extant dress, costume, textiles and accessories were added to the drive from the museum visits.

The resource list is now housed on the CalArts Library database website https://library.calarts.edu/az.php, under the title CalArts Resource List for Diversity, Equity, Accessibility, and Inclusion in Dress, Fashion, and Costume.

Table 3.1 Syllabus Calendar

Week	Class Topic
Week 1	First Class: Introduction Course introduction, overview, requirements, student introductions Discussion: How and why are equity, diversity, access and inclusivity in fashion history important?
Week 2	Ancient Egypt Cultural exchange, trade, and cities in the ancient world
Week 3	Ancient Greece and Rome Weaving, textiles, looms, and draping; social hierarchy and gender roles Group research project: Ancient dress
Week 4	Persia and the Byzantine Period The rise of the Christian Church, the age of Persian craft, and Byzantine culture Fashion case study: The Met Museum Gala "Heavenly Creatures"
Week 5	Medieval times and the Ottoman Empire The Crusades, the Bubonic Plague, Ottoman Empire conquests Selected readings – "Fashion in the Age of the Black Prince"
Week 6	The Renaissance and scientific thinking The concept of "the other", how fashion reinforces difference, early science Group study project: The Renaissance/world-building exercise
Week 7	16th century: Queen Elizabeth and the New World Supply and demand, trade routes, colonization, indigenous cultures The Cotton Triangle, the Age of Conquest, and other terrible human ideas

Week	Class Topic
Week 8	17th century: Europe, Africa, and India Colonialism and fashion, India's influence on textile trade and design African natural resources; Dutch, Portuguese, and English goods
Week 9	18th century: Europe, America, and the Black diaspora Western tailoring practices, the silk trade, the Grand Tour History of headwraps, denim, and Black civil rights carnival costume as protest
Week 10	19th century: The Victorians and Japonisme The Industrial Revolution, cultural appropriation, uniformity in menswear Japan, Victorian England, the fin de siècle, the Great Renunciation
Week 11	20th century: Fashion, war, and globalization War, fashion, nationalism, social control, paranoia, and propaganda Subcultures, zoot suits, cholas, Harlem renaissance, punks, art
Week 12	21st century: Post-modernism, disruption, and fragmentation Extreme fashion, gender identity and dress, street style, social media, nudity What is the future of fashion? Who are the new industry influencers?
Week 13	Last class: Group study project presentations

Source: Camille Benda, 2022

The throughline of this class is rigorous questioning of the white Western default in traditional art history. How can we gain valuable information through the lens of dress, fashion, and clothing? Throughout the semester, students learn to reframe the contributions of underserved and underrepresented groups to the history of clothing, fashion, costume, and adornment. For example, while studying the French Revolution, students research the Chevalier D'Eon, a middle-class military veteran and expert fencer who presented as a man in his early years but dressed, lived, and died as a woman in his later years. Through the study of this unique story, students learn the basics of 18th-century Western dress for men and women through the Chevalier, who wore both. Although on the surface, early portraits of the Chevalier D'Eon show a typically white, male, middle-class sitter, students can explore a much deeper story and understand the gender expression and social class shown through fashion. Looking at dress is a survey not only of how we wear garments but also of how we behave as a society and how we assign values and morals to individuals. Clothing is truly a very personal, intimate way of looking at history.

Starting From a Basic Vocabulary

Throughout Conscious Fashion History, emphasis is placed on developing a student's communication skills and enhancing their ability to read about, critically analyze, and write about dress and fashion. While learning the basic classic dress history terms (for instance, in Ancient Greece: Chiton, peplos, himation, chlamys, fillet), students focus on their social, political, and cultural significance. At the beginning of the semester, the class does a group exercise reflecting the introduction in *Fashion History: A Global View* by Abby Lillethun and Linda Welters to investigate what the differences are between primary dress history definitions, like dress versus fashion, clothing versus adornment, mode versus habit, and more.

Course Projects and Assessment

Assessment for this course includes individual and group research projects, in-class exercises, student participation in class, attendance, and a final fashion history paper. The class meets once a week, and students are expected to work independently on their homework and be prepared to present in class.

15%, 4 Mood Board Projects, 17th–20th Century Fashion: Students will be assigned 4 5-page mood board projects, in which they document each century of fashion through one global location (1600s, 1700s, 1800s, 1900s) by researching and showing unique images (images that have not already

Table 3.2 Course Assessment

20%	Participation, Discussion
15%	4 Mood Board Projects, 17th–20th-Century Fashion
15%	Group Research Project: Ancient World Dress
20%	Group Study Project: The Renaissance/World-Building Exercise
30%	Final Fashion History Paper

been shown in lectures). Each mood board will be introduced by a 1-page bullet-point overview of the social, cultural, and political forces that shaped that century.

15%, Group Research Project: Ancient World Dress: Students will work in teams of 4, studying an assigned ancient city, its inhabitants, and what they would have worn, paying particular attention to historical facts regarding the ethnic/racial diversity of their assigned city. They will create a 1-page board and 1-page overview, 500 words, for a 10-minute presentation to the class.

20%, Group Study Project: The Renaissance/World-Building Exercise: Working in different groups, students will tackle equitable investigation into fashion history, which relies on going beyond the basic research (which usually focuses on the rich, the well documented, and the powerful). While many underrepresented groups have almost been wiped from the stage of significance, it is possible to find documentation, but it takes more time to find. The Renaissance project will be an exercise in learning how to look deeply to find diverse representation. Students will deconstruct a Renaissance painting, break down the subjects, and find parallel research to document what nationalities and cultural groups existed in society at that time. Students will learn how to use a circular "windmill of research" rather than a linear way of looking at history.

30%, Final Fashion History Paper (2,500-word essay): Synthesize what students have learned into a final paper that focuses on developing their own original opinions on a specific point in fashion history that they feel is relevant to de-colonizing and reframing how we look at clothing, diversity, inclusion, and equity. Using texts, art historical references, and articles, students will reflect on how cultural appropriation and racism affect our view of art and design.

Sample Project

Sample Project

The goal of this project, assigned during the 4th week of the course, was to inspire students to see the ancient world (Ancient Egypt, Persia, Greece, Rome, and Northern Europe) as interconnected, dynamic trading partners. Students were encouraged to explore how different cultural groups would have interacted, culminating in the study of how Norse and Persian dress had striking similarities in pattern making. Students presented their work in groups, and each student chose a role in their particular group: For instance, navigator, leader, healer, translator, cook.

> Assignment prompt: You are a group of ancient traders (anywhere from 10,000 BCE – 1 CE) who are setting off from Persia to the Norse lands to trade. You are working together, but each of you has a distinct role: For instance, navigator, craftsperson, trader, caretaker, negotiator, manager, etc. Figure out what time period you are in, what Persian goods you are trading, what your route is, what you bring with you (include what you are all wearing), and what you want to get from the Norse countries to bring back home. Other topics to look at: What/who do you encounter on the way? What challenges do you face? Do any of your crew stay behind to live somewhere along the way to start a new life? Presentations can be digital or hard copy, including visuals and bullet-point text. Presentations should be 5 to 10 minutes long, and each student should present a portion of the assignment.
>
> *Source*: Camille Benda, 2022

Tying It Together

Traditional dress history has typically focused heavily on Western European subjects, people of privilege, and often white sitters, but that is changing. Waiting around the corner of many famous paintings or photographs are sitters of color, non-Western subjects, and LGBTQIA+ individuals. Historic events are not changing through this research, but the perception and analysis of the events can change; it is a matter of trying to present a wider spectrum of images than is typically available in the canon of Western dress history research. In Conscious Fashion History class, research focuses on a society or culture as a whole, a circle, and looks at the totality of its members, rather than at the most famous or wealthiest at the top of the pyramid.

In the School of Theatre at CalArts, students are trained to be artist activists and change makers. In the past few years, a watershed in representation has revolutionized stage and screen, and artists of the future want to be equipped in a diverse and robust way. Once students graduate and become emerging professionals in the field, they have the opportunity to influence casting by showing inclusive research to directors, to tackle challenges around cultural appropriation through historical analysis, and inspire to actors with concrete and equitable sketches and images that represent a 3-dimensional character.

> **Choosing Materials for Reference and Discussion**
>
> During the process of creating this new class, I developed a list of notes that helped define which images, books, articles, and journals were chosen for the curriculum. Some of the main questions here still form the core of how the class investigates a particular painting, time period, or historical document:
>
> - We are part of a cultural continuum – we hope to add to fashion history but acknowledge that this is a work in progress, not an end point.
> - We understand that fashion/dress history is a developing field, only 100–150 years old, so terminology is still new. Researchers have the chance to add and improve terminology and language around dress history, inclusivity, diversity, and equity.
> - We as researchers consciously or unconsciously apply "filters" to all materials we search:
> - What are the "typical" filters for dress history?
> - What filters can we change?
> - What filters can we apply to be more inclusive?
> - Who gets to decide which images we include in a dress history survey?
> - Who traditionally is the gatekeeper for dress history scholarship?
> - Who was the ruling party at any given point in history, who were the oppressed, and how does that affect perception?
> - How do we separate fact from myth in image research?
>
> *Source*: Camille Benda, 2022

Hands-on 3D work is essential to interdisciplinary study at CalArts and for understanding clothing on the human body. In the 6th week of Conscious Fashion History, students conclude their studies of the ancient world by dividing into groups of 4 to 6 in the costume shop and working with textiles and mannequins to drape, pleat, cut, wrap, pin, and fasten garments documented in different dress history books. In the 2022 fall semester, students created looks from ancient Mesopotamia, Egypt, Greece, Persia, Rome, and Norse dress. Students were most fascinated by the Ancient Egyptian gazelle skin loincloth they recreated from Blanche Payne's 1965 book "History of Costume".

During the 18th-century week, the class researched the dynamic landscape of French Revolutionary dress, from rich to poor, young to old, through primary sources and respected publications. This allowed students to see how understanding all social classes, gender expressions, and political views gave them a much fuller picture of fashion than just internet research or Pinterest boards. The final class included a student self-portrait collage of how they think they would have dressed during the French Revolution. Students were encouraged throughout the class to becoming budding dress historians themselves and to develop their own opinions on a moment in history.

It has been so gratifying to see students respond to the course material and to incorporate physical research into their digital work, especially coming out of pandemic learning, when digital was the only approach. During the semester, students were highly encouraged to bring in 5 books from the library each week on the topic at hand. Students also got familiar with critiquing books and asking questions about the equity, diversity, and inclusivity in older publications. One session in class included group work looking at books before the 1960s and determining what terminology and perspectives had changed. Suddenly, students had ownership of this material and could dialogue with it, rather than completing a passive reading assignment.

Finally, it was thrilling to see students develop a sense of humor and curiosity about fashion history topics. Since art is sometimes seen as inaccessible and elitist, it was important to show students that clothing is incredibly personal and relevant to all. Finding connections between past fashions and the fashions of today meant that students became closer to the source material and saw the sitters in paintings as fellow humans.

4

Fashion Forward

A History of Dress in Global Context

Julie Leavitt Learson

This course examines the way in which clothes are tools of identity and power by exploring dress and adornment from around the world. The history of dress is the story of humanity; how we choose to decorate our bodies is an expression of who we are, where we see ourselves in our community, and how our fellow humans view us. Through readings, discussions, research, writings, and creative projects, students will deepen their understanding of how clothing can empower individuals, make subtle statements, exert cultural supremacy, and support social hierarchies.

The course is divided into an introduction week and three modules. Each module includes an overarching theme and a few smaller sub-categories. Modules begin with a lecture/discussion slide show juxtaposing images of extant garments and artifacts with fashionably dressed people in artwork and media, from different places and times related to the theme. The lecture day also includes historical maps and other supporting materials. Students then read short articles or book excerpts on the topic and discuss them in class in small groups and as a class. Each module section wraps up with a short research project based on the theme.

The course culminates in a final project: Conceiving of a museum exhibition on a fashion history topic through a social justice lens. Students are to research their topic, find artefacts and art images to include, and develop a slide show presentation and scripted audio tour that takes people through their imagined showcase.

> School: Fairfield University
>
> Department: Theatre (cross-listed with Art History)
>
> Student Level/Description: Upper-level undergraduate course open to all majors
>
> Class Size: 25 maximum
>
> Hours/Week: 2.5
>
> Format: In person
>
> Text or Core Materials:
>
> Benda, Camille. *Dressing the Resistance: The Visual Language of Protest Through History*, Princeton Architectural Press, 2021.
>
> Ford, Richard Thompson. *Dress Codes: How the Laws of Fashion Made History*, Simon & Schuster, 2021.
>
> Welters, Linda and Abby Lillethun. *Fashion History: A Global View*, Bloomsbury Visual Arts, 2018.
>
> Additional articles and book excerpts from a variety of sources.
>
> Types of Access Needed: Library, internet, digital museum archives

Making the Change

In the summer of 2020, our university theatre program, like so many other theatrical and academic institutions, felt called to meaningfully respond to the Black Lives Matter movement. This moment of change came as I finished a semester teaching a traditional fashion history course: The steady parade of European silhouettes from Ancient Greece through the mid-20th century. It was a solid grounding in traditional subject framing. But I was dissatisfied with my current fashion history course content, and I had used my time during the first summer of the pandemic to take seminars and workshops on the teaching of costume history in the 21st century, collaborating with costume professors and practitioners on how to revise coursework for students interested in the wider world beyond Europe.

As I was rethinking my pedagogical goals, our college announced a new "Magis Core" curriculum, which included a social justice signature curriculum element. As stated in the university handbook, "[D]esignated SJ courses accomplish the learning outcomes through a focus on race, broadly construed, studied intersectionality with gender and class." This college-wide paradigm shift aligned with my personal teaching goals.

Fairfield University is a Jesuit institution, dedicated to the tradition of *cura personalis* – care for the body, mind, and spirit of each student – where, according to our mission, teachers work to "develop the creative and intellectual potential of students" and where "the promotion of justice is an absolute requirement" for students and educators alike. Empathy has been a core teaching principle in both my theatre production and costume coursework. With a directive from the university to develop coursework that focused on issues of race, gender, and class in order to "prepare young men and women for others," I was ready to create an empathy-driven, inclusive, fashion history curriculum, in which students explored the socio-economic whys and hows behind fashion trends.

Our theatre major is a small BA program. Our pedagogy is liberal arts oriented, not conservatory focused. Most students in our theatre classes are non-majors seeking an arts credit. A course that appeals to a wide range of majors and minors would mean moving away from an industry-specific focus while still teaching content that spoke to my passions and fueled my research.

This new course focus also allowed me to make a case for fashion and costume studies to be taken more seriously as an area of academic interest. Every costume designer knows their work involves knowledge of and crossover research into any number of other fields–world history, economics, psychology, chemistry, art history, religious studies, garment construction, literature, material culture, politics, gender studies, physics, mythology, etc. However, most people who are not costume designers or technicians themselves sometimes assume that costumes just . . . magically *appear* on actors at dress rehearsal. The work of creating costumes is routinely dismissed as "just shopping" or "arts and crafts" by people who don't take into account the vast skill set required to create well-researched, meaningful, and creative costumes.

To create successful costumes, one must study fashion history, and to study fashion history is to study humanity. Getting dressed is a single act that virtually every human being engages in on a daily basis and has for millennia. What we wear, how we adorn our bodies, and why we choose particular articles of dress are in part determined by our gender, age, ethnicity, religion, personality, history, socio-economic status, health, mood, and occupation. Fashion can dovetail with almost any major in a university catalogue. The fashion industry is a global, multi-billion-dollar economic force. Yet "fashion" is often dismissed as a frivolous hobby for unserious people who don't need a "real job." (The gender, race, and class biases bound up in this perception are hard to ignore.)

As part of this course, I wanted to remind students just how integral fashion is to our lives, in both positive and negative ways. Fashion reshapes both the global economy and local economies over and over again. It impacts the environment for good and for ill. It can be a tool for personal expression of

Figure 4.1 "The Invention of the Suit," slide from "Cultural Borrowing, Appreciation, and Appropriation" lecture

political oppression. It creates jobs and exploits labor. It defines – or subverts – gender and religious and cultural norms. It sparks revolutions and riots. All this is worth studying, and framing fashion in this context is much more exciting and meaningful to me than memorizing the chronological progression of the shifting fashionable silhouette.

I was eager to create a course that not only broadened students' knowledge base but also increased their empathy and expanded their understanding of their fellow humans. I wanted to develop content and ideas that students could take beyond the classroom and into their future lives as citizens, community members, and consumers of fashion. In so doing, I was serving the Jesuit mission of our university and honoring the call to decolonize our curriculum.

Course Objectives
- ◆ To explore the power of fashion on personal and cultural identity by making meaningful connections between fashion artworks and other examples of human expression within their historical contexts;

- To identify intersecting systems of power through the history of fashionable dress, including race, class, ethnicity, gender, sex and sexuality, and religion; and
- To analyze critical questions about assumptions, biases, and world views on how fashion can continue to empower people in a post-colonial society.

Learning Outcomes

By the end of this course, you will have been taught to:

- Analyze critical questions about assumptions, biases, and world-views on how fashion can continue to empower or oppress people in a post-colonial society;
- Demonstrate understanding of the historical and/or contemporary context of power, inequity, and oppression in fashion history;
- Articulate orally and in writing how social identities and cultural values intersect to influence different worldviews and experiences in a global society through dress and adornment;
- Analyze your own social identities, cultural values, and privilege as expressed in clothing;
- Explore answers to critical social questions from multiple perspectives;
- Recognize historic roots of contemporary styles and identify the cultures of origin in extant articles of fashion;
- Become conversant in fashion history and textile terms;
- Efficiently find, evaluate, cite, and use sources, including museum objects and online images to research fashion history, makers, and objects;
- Impactfully present findings in appropriate written, visual, and oral form; and
- Think mindfully about personal fashion choices and consumer behavior.

The first week, students are introduced to fashion and textile terms via excerpts from Linda Welters and Abby Lillethun's *Fashion History: A Global View*. They then discuss:

- What is "fashion"?
- What is a "costume"?
- How might fashion manifest itself on a human body?
- What can fashion choices tell us about the wearer?

Table 4.1 Syllabus Calendar, Spring 2022

Module	Week	Content	Assignment Due
The Roots of Fashion	1: What Is Fashion?	Watch: *The West Wing* (clip); *The Devil Wears Prada* (clip) Assign: Initial Reflection	
		Slide show presentation: Fashion and textile terms Read: Welters and Lillethun, *Fashion History A Global View* (Chapter 2)	Initial Reflection due
	2: Fashion and the Environment	Slide show: India, Egypt, China, Greece, the Incas, and Hawaii Read: Burnham, Dorothy, *Cut My Cote*; Barber, Elizabeth Wayland, *Women's Work* (excerpt) Assign: Historic Garment Analysis	
		Read: Ganz, Grace, "How Fast Fashion Causes Environmental Poverty"; Gorvit, Zaria, "The Ancient Fabric That No One Knows How to Make"; Sawai, Akshay, "The Devil Wears Vegan Leather"	Historic Garment Analysis
Fashion and Socio-Economic Power	3: Sumptuary Laws and Dress Codes	Slide show: Medieval Europe, Feudal Japan (Tokugawa period), Korea (Joseon Dynasty), China (Han dynasty), 19th century American South Assign: Status Symbols Poster	

		Read: Ford, Richard Thompson, *Dress Codes* (excerpt); Postrel, Virginia I. *The Fabric of Civilization* (excerpt)	
	4: Cotton and Enslavement	Read: Shaw, Madelyn, "Slave Cloth and Clothing Slaves" Guest lecturer Cheyney McKnight of Not Your Mama's History, "A Story in the Threads"	
		Read: Cottom, Tressie McMillan, "Why Do Poor People 'Waste' Money on Luxury Goods?"	Status Symbols Poster
	5: Fashion and Cultural Appropriation	Slide show: Jacobean/Restoration; Persia; First Nations; Japanese kimono Assign: Appropriation/Appreciation Case Study	
		Read: Jirousek, Charlotte with Sara Catterall, *Ottoman Dress and Design in the West* (excerpt); Deloria, Philip J., *Playing Indian* (excerpt); Said, Edward W. *Orientalism* (excerpt); Banerjee, Mukulika and Daniel Miller. *The Sari* (excerpt)	
	6: Fashion and Cultural Appropriation	No Class	
		Read: Carriger, Michelle Liu, "No Thing to Wear"	Appropriation/ Appreciation Case Study

(*Continued*)

Table 4.1 Continued

Module	Week	Content	Assignment Due
Fashion and Individual Expression	7: Fashion and Gender	Slide show: Tudor; Victorian; gender in dress Assign: Ungendered Fashion Design Project	
		Watch: TEDxUMN, Nick Metcalf, "Two Spirits" video clip; TEDx "Filipino Gender Fluidity" video clip	
	8: Fashion and Gender	Read: Mohanty, Chandra T., *Third World Women and the Politics of Feminism* (excerpt); Halberstam, Jack, *Female Masculinity* (excerpt): Mersmann, Birgit, "Remodeling the Past, Cross-dressing the Future" Listen: "(De)Gendered Fashion: Past, Present and Future with Alok Vaid-Menon, Part I," *Dressed* podcast	
		Slide show: Baroque/Puritan, Victorian, Revolutionary Iran, Dia de los Muertos, Madonna	Ungendered Fashion Design Project
	9	Spring Break	
		Spring Break	
	10: Fashion and Faith	Final Project Q&A; Library session with reference librarian	

11: Fashion and Faith	Read: Ford, Richard Thompson. *Dress Codes* (Chapter 3, "Signs of Faith"; Chapter 15. "Piercing the Veil"); "The Veiling Issue in 20th Century Iran"	
12: Fashion as Political Statement	Slide show: 18th-century France, 20th-century America: Suffragettes, zoot suits, flower power, Black is beautiful, fashionable Filipinas	
13: Fashion as Political Statement	Meet individually to discuss final project	
	Meet individually to discuss final project	Final project progress report
14: Fashion as Political Statement	Read: Ford, Richard Thompson, *Dress Codes* (Chapter 11: "From Rags to Resistance"); Benda, Camille, *Dressing the Resistance* (excerpt); Werlin, Katie, "The Chemise a la Reine"	
	Read: Ford, Tanisha C., "Imagining Africa," in *Liberated Threads: Black Women, Style, and the Global Politics of Soul*; Bennett, Brad, "The CROWN Act Movement . . ." Assign: Rebellious Fashion Poster Design	
	No Class	

(Continued)

Table 4.1 Continued

Module	Week	Content	Assignment Due
	15: Fashion and Post-Colonial Identity	Read: McGowan, Amanda, "Iconic 'Ghana Must Go' Bag Gets Refashioned as a Meditation on Migration"; Mentges, Gabriele, "Reviewing Orientalism and Reorienting Fashion Beyond Europe"; Frankland, Claire, "World AIDS Day: The Red Ribbon"	
		Read: Lieber, Chavie, "The Reclaiming of Native American Dress"; McConnell, Kyra, "The Importance of Frida Kahlo's Clothes"	Rebellious Fashion Poster Project
	16: Fashion and Post-Colonial Identity	Slide show: *Hamilton* (Paul Tazewell, inspired in part by Kehinde Wiley); Afrofuturism in *Black Panther* (Ruth E. Carter); *Jingle Jangle: A Christmas Journey* (Michael Wilkinson) Read: Eisman, Sonja, "Afrofuturism as a Strategy for Decolonizing the Global Fashion Archive"	
		Making sense of the semester; final project Q & A	
	Final Exam	Present final projects	

Source: Julie Learson

A short self-reflection assignment accompanies this introductory unit. Students are tasked with assembling their favorite outfit – garments, footwear, accessories – and taking a photo of themselves wearing it. They then answer a series of questions to inspire reflection on their outfit choice:

- Why did they choose this particular collection of items?
- How did this ensemble make the wearer feel?
- What did the wearer hope to communicate with their choices?

Next, students are asked to investigate – as much as is possible – where their items came from.

- What are they made of?
- Who might have made them?
- How did the items come to be part of their own wardrobes?

Finally, students share details about their outfits with the class. They start discussing the complicated global network that feeds the fashion industry: "Fast fashion," "heirlooms," "upcycling," labor practices, carbon footprints, and environmental impact. They also note some common themes as well as differences among the outfits.

- Does our campus have a specific "look"?
- Did students come to campus with that look, or did they adapt their taste to fit in (or to stand out)?
- Do students who don't follow a popular trend feel welcomed or judged for nonconformity?
- Do students find themselves making assumptions about their peers based on their outfits?
- Are these assumptions confirmed or upended when students get to know each other?
- What might all this say about our campus culture?

This transitions into the first module: The Roots of Fashion. Students explore traditional textiles from several ancient cultures – linen in Egypt, wool in the Andes, silk in China, and cotton in India – and how each of these cultures wove these locally sourced materials into textiles, which were then shaped into traditional garments. The class discusses how labor (Who was making these textiles? How long did it take to make them?), innovation (How were these garments from different parts of the world similar? How were they distinct?), and the environment (Why were certain materials and techniques used or avoided?) all had hands in creating these garments. They study Dorothy Burnham's *Cut My Cote* to understand how different peoples have ingeniously and efficiently cut these long rectangles of cloth into similarly shaped yet culturally distinct garments. They also look at methods of draping or pleating cloth into equally distinct garments from saris to kilts. Students are asked to observe and discuss different weaving patterns and embellishment techniques, including dyeing, printing, and embroidery. Juxtaposed with images from the past, students read about contemporary challenges and potential solutions: Labor practices in the textile industry, the environmental impact of fast fashion, the revival of a nearly extinct textile material, and the development of potentially new, sustainable textiles.

The accompanying assignment helps students hone their research and attribution skills. After finding several examples of t-shaped, draped, or wrapped garments in museum collection databases, students look for echoes of these ancient articles of dress in contemporary fashionable garments.

They are asked to consider:

- How is the twenty-first century interpreting traditional silhouettes, shapes, textiles, techniques, and design motifs?
- How have manufacture and labor practices changed?
- What might these choices say about contemporary values and taste?

The second module, Fashion and Socio-Economic Power, is divided into three sections. Students first look at sumptuary laws and dress codes, comparing medieval Europe, Japan during the Edo period, the Joseon Dynasty in Korea, and the Han Dynasty of China. They read excerpts from Richard Thompson's *Dress Codes*. They discuss how fashionable dress can communicate wealth, class, and other hierarchal status traits and think of examples of contemporary status symbols. They are then given randomly chosen fashion status symbols from a variety of places and times and give a short presentation on the item in question and its significance to its community.

In the second section of this module, the class takes a deeper dive into the intersection of fashion status, the cotton trade, and enslavement. Students learn about the cultures and fashion practices of several West African peoples and consider how they might have tried to hold on to their dress traditions after being taken to the Americas. They look briefly at European fashions in the Americas and Europe of the 17th and 18th century and read Madelyn Shaw's web article "Slave Cloth and Clothing Slaves" to understand how the plantation system clothed its enslaved workers. They hear from historical interpreter Cheyney McKnight of Not Your Momma's History, look at portraits, and read descriptions of enslaved and free Africans in the Americas.

They consider:

- How might these people have viewed themselves?
- How might others have viewed them?
- How could fashion express identity even under extreme coercive social pressure?
- Could fashion serve as a means of cultural assimilation, or did certain people find themselves forever in violation of ever-shifting "rules" of "appropriate" dress?

Students wrap this section up considering the persistent echoes of fashion laws, codes, and status by discussing Tressie McMillan Cottom's article "Why Do Poor People 'Waste' Money on Luxury Goods?"

The third part of this module addresses cultural appropriation and fashion. Students look at the influence of Persian, Ottoman, Indian, and Asian fashions on European taste. They read excerpts from Edward W. Said's *Orientalism*, Philip Deloria's *Playing Indian*, Charlotte Jirousek and Sara Catterall's *Ottoman Dress and Design in the West*, and other texts that showcase the "othering" of non-European cultures, even as Europeans "borrow" these cultures' textiles, garments, and ornaments.

They wrestle with the concept of cultural appropriation:

- Is there a clear definition, or is it a "we'll know it when we see it" idea?
- Where is the line between "appreciation" and "appropriation?"
- Who decides when it has been crossed?
- Can instances of cultural appropriation be remedied?

Students research contemporary cases of potential appropriation, analyze the details, and offer alternative ways to handle each situation. Students finish this section with Michele Liu Carrier's article, "No Thing to Wear," which analyzes a complicated public controversy about a kimono-themed exhibit at Boston's Museum of Fine Arts.

It is at this point that students start serious work on their final project: Presenting an idea for an imagined museum exhibition with a fashion and social justice theme. (See Figure 4.4) In addition to thoroughly investigating their chosen topic, students are asked to consider the following as they develop their presentations:

- What would people see or experience?
- How would the information and artefacts be presented?

- How might visitors interact with the materials?
- What would patrons take with them from this experience?

Students have been encouraged to think up topics from the beginning of the semester – each content area has a "Want to learn more?" section in the syllabus, with a short list of tangential subjects not covered in class – and have had at least one meeting with the professor to discuss their ideas. An example of a completed assignment is in the syllabus. By now, students are expected to have chosen a topic and started preliminary research. The work begins in earnest with a visit to our campus library for a guided workshop with our class librarian. During this workshop, students complete short research tasks using different library resources, including Artstor, Credo, online databases, and book searches. They then engage in individual research for their final projects.

The last module of the course, Fashion and Individual Expression, focuses on fashion as a tool of identity and empowerment. This module is also broken down into three smaller sub-sections. The first section focuses on fashion and gender. Students compare fashions of the Tudor and Victorian periods with the Wakashu of Edo-era Japan, Two-Spirit people in Native American cultures, the Hijra in India, the Fa'afafine and Fa'afatame of Samoa, the Muxes of Mexico, and the Bakla of the Philippines. They then talk about gender identity and fashion today. Resources include slide shows, readings, TED Talks (Nick Metcalf, "Why We Need Gender Fluidity"; Frances Villarta, "The Gender Fluid History of the Philippines"), and podcasts (Dressed: "(De)Gendered Fashion: Past, Present and Future with Alok Vaid-Menon, Parts I and II").

Students wrestle with questions like:

- What does it mean to appear "masculine" or "feminine" (or neither)?
- How have the concepts of gender and gendered fashion changed over time and place?
- Why do/do we need to identify our gender through fashion?

This section ends with students imagining a nonbinary fashion design look, which, according to students, is both the most popular and the most challenging assignment of the semester.

The second section briefly explores fashion's connection with religious practices and professions of faith. Students look at civilian religious dress among contemporary devout Jewish, Muslim, Sikh, and Christian communities, unpacking the significance of veiling, modest dress, hairstyles, and other significant symbols of faith. They discuss laws that promote or suppress specific articles of dress among religious practitioners:

- Who do these laws serve?
- How do people within and outside these communities feel about their dress codes?
- Can one be "religious" and "fashionable" at the same time?
- Should there be secular laws that govern religious expression in dress?

The final section of the module takes a look at fashion as a political statement. After reading sections of Camille Benda's *Dressing the Resistance* and Richard Thompson's *Dress Codes*, students compare fashions worn by French revolutionaries in the late 18th century to those of zoot suiters, civil rights activists, and Black Panthers in mid-20th century America.

- How did these groups use their clothing, hair styles, and accessories to communicate with each other, the public, the media?
- How did the public at large respond?
- How did/did these looks and/or their symbolic significance change over time?

Students then research another "fashion rebel" or iconic "rebellious" fashion item of their choosing from global history and present their findings to the class.

The last weeks of class focus on Fashion and Post-Colonial Identity. Students read articles including Chavie Lieber's "The Reclaiming of Native American Dress," Kyra McConnell's "The Importance of Frida Kahlo's Clothes," Gabriele Mentges's "Reviewing Orientalism," and Adti Mayer's "Decolonizing Fashion." Students discuss these answers to the historic impacts of colonialism, imperialism, and white supremacy and think of other ways that fashion could empower members of the global majority.

The course ends with a discussion of Afrofuturism. Students read Sonja Eisman's article "Afrofuturism as a Strategy for Decolonizing the Global Fashion Archive," explore the work of several Afrofuturist fashion designers and artists through Connie Wang's interviews on Refinery 29, and discuss how Afrofuturism infuses the work of costume designers Ruth E. Carter (*Black Panther*), Paul Tazewell (*Hamilton*), and Michael Wilkinson (*Jingle Jangle: A Christmas Journey*). Students discuss the impact of colonization, racism, sexism, and classism on this fashion trend and how different consumers respond to it.

The class then opines on the future of fashion:

- Where might fashion go from here?
- Will fashion serve as a tool of oppression or liberation?
- Will consumerism continue to generate mass pollution and waste, or will sustainability become the new chic?
- Will fashion become more diverse or more conforming?

Student Historic Garment Project: "Kimono Then & Now," by Reese Giordano

This kimono is constructed of silk and embroidered silk, with hand-painted motifs all around. The silk fabric was created via weaving. The purple cloth has the hand-painted pine on it, and the white plums were embroidered on the back. Like the kimono in *Cut My Cote* on page 30, I believe this kimono was made from long rectangular shapes of fabric that were sewn together to produce the kimono. In *Cut My Cote*, there are three long rectangles and two shorter rectangles, one thicker than the other. The outline of the sewing line where the textiles are sewed together can be seen along the longer pieces of cloth. The women's kimono in *Cut My Cote* and the kimono at the Met are composed of silk and feature embroidery. They are both designed to be floor length. The women's kimono has stenciled patterning, whereas the Met kimono does not. The designs on the Met kimono are the distinguishing features that help identify this as being produced for Japanese society. The Three Friends of Winter (*shōchikubai*) – pine, bamboo, and plum – are included in the description, as is the garment's title. It discusses the significance of each plant, with the pine signifying longevity and renewal, the bamboo indicating endurance and strength, and the plum being the first bloom of spring and epitomizing nature's renewal. Despite their origins in China, these designs have a long history in Japanese textile art (Metropolitan Museum of Art).

To construct the lovely designs visible on the garment, I imagine it would have been very time consuming, and I would have had to be very meticulous with my weaving, stitching, and hand painting. In the end, I would have been very proud of my work because the symbols it depicts have so much meaning in Japanese and Chinese culture. I would also like to consider that almost none of my fabric has gone to waste. I do not believe the wearer and the creator are the same person because this is a high-end kimono that took a lot of time and effort to make. The wearer must have paid for this to be made for them by someone with a lot of talent. Because of the silk fabric, I would feel luxurious wearing this kimono. It would be really elegant and comfortable to wear. This looks like it might be a daily outfit for someone with a high social rank in Japan. This garment demonstrates your wealth and prosperity.

I discovered a comparable garment in contemporary fashion, the Barbara tiered-lace kimono, on the Free People website. Unlike the Japanese kimono, the modern one is considered an accessory; it is likewise made of a sheer cloth and features lace details. Both have flowy sleeves and, due to their loose fit, do not provide a human figure silhouette. Both contain floral designs throughout the fabric, but the prints on Japanese kimonos have cultural symbolism. The Free People kimono is made from a polyamide fabric which is "a flexible synthetic fiber, also known as nylon" while the Japanese kimono is made of silk fabric (the Laundress). The modern garment was made in the United States and was most likely mass produced in vast facilities across many states. The Japanese kimono, on the other hand, was handcrafted for a specific customer who is the sole owner of this specific kimono.

Figure 4.2 Kimono with pines, bamboo, and plum, Japan, 1926–1950, artist unknown; Barbara lace-tiered kimono, Free People, style no. 62383161, United States, 2022

Sources: The Metropolitan Museum of Art, Accession Number 2013.510.4, www.metmuseum.org/art/collection/search/76985, accessed January, 26 2022; Free People, Spring Line, 2022.

Table 4.2 Historic Garment Analysis Project Rubric (10% of course grade)

	Missed the Mark 0–5	**Got the Gist 6–8**	**Crushed It! 9–10**
This project featured an appropriate historical garment (10%).			
This project featured an appropriate contemporary garment (10%).			
This project properly cited its sources (10%).			
This project thoughtfully answered the questions posed in the instructions (15%).			
This paper was well written, well organized, and interesting to read (15%).			
This project's visual component was appropriate, informative, creative, and neat (15%).			
This project made appropriate and informed use of vocabulary terms (15%).			
This paper showed good writing mechanics, spelling, punctuation, and grammar (10%).			

> I created a "Want more?" section in each module folder. There I listed topics related to the module that we didn't cover in class.
>
> **I included:**
> - Titles of books and articles;
> - Names of prominent people, communities, and events;
> - Museum exhibits and artifacts;
> - Inventions or techniques related to garment construction;
> - Video links; and
> - Vocabulary terms.
>
> This gave students a wealth of possible final project topics that wouldn't be recycled from course content.

Sample Student Assignment: "Ungendered Fashion Design," by Natalia Kotowska

Outfit Description:
This outfit is something I would like to see someone wearing as street fashion in New York City or even on a runway. Beginning at the top, the model has a slick man bun and is wearing rectangular sunglasses. They also have a dangly diamond earing in their ear. Their blouse is satin and features a flowy fabric with a white bow necktie. The pants are knee length structured leather pants, with the material giving a more rectangular silhouette to the outfit. The pants are also high waisted, outlining a slimmer-appearing waist. The chain belt is tied around the waist but is clipped loosely and not close to the body, to give a dangling appearance. The outfit also features distressed black sheer stockings. The shoes are Gucci loafers. The final accessory is a singlet ring featuring an onyx stone, worn on the thumb. I chose to put together this outfit because it uses elements of more "female fashion" with fabrics such as silk and satin with more "male fashion" materials, such as leather and distressed fabrics. This outfit is a neutral color as well, with small color detail added with gold jewelry. The flowy top and structured pants juxtapose each other, shaping the body in a way that does not shift focus to masculine or feminine features or body parts. The only part of the body that is accentuated is the

Figure 4.3 Sample student assignment: "Ungendered Fashion Design," by Natalia Kotowska

waist with the high-waisted pants. The long hair in a slicked-back bun is a feminine hairstyle that slicks back the face and expresses higher cheekbones and a stronger facial structure that is more often associated with men.

Collage captions:
1. Tux dress: I picked this dress because it has a silhouette of both a dress and a tux. The collar of the dress has the same details as a tux while the bottom of the dress is a skirt.
2. This outfit is being worn by a male model but includes feminine fashion attributes such as satin pants and flowy fabrics. It also includes the structure that is seen in male attire with the trouser pants. Lastly, it is white, which I more often associate with female clothing.
3. I chose this sheer organza top because the fabric reminds me of many female blouses; however, it's being worn by a male model.

4. I chose this ring because it is gold and black onyx. I chose this ring because I feel as though gold is a unisex metal, but the black onyx is more of a male metal.
5. Shorts and high socks were featured in the Gucci fashion show as shown with this image clip. It also reminds me of schoolgirl outfits consisting of skirts and knee-high socks.
6. Gucci loafers are very popular amongst both genders. I own these shoes, and so do my uncle and a few of my male friends.
7. I chose this Hermes briefcase because of its structured shape, along with the taupe color. I feel as though the color is popular among both genders, and both genders utilize briefcases.
8. This black trench coat is unisex as it features a structures silhouette as seen in male outfits, along with a belt to add a cinched waist, as seen in female outfits.
9. The man bun is picking up popularity in both male and female outfits. A slicked-back bun is very fashionable when it comes to women's fashion, and the man bun is a newer trend.
10. I feel as though a leather jacket is a staple in both male and female closets. I often see designer leather jackets being unisex, like the ACME jacket I chose to include.
11. I chose this gold chain because it is a staple in my jewelry collection, as well as in those of many of my male friends. Gold is a unisex metal, in my opinion.
12. I chose these pants because they have a neutral color. Furthermore, they have a structured trouser shape associated with a men's suit, but it has a more tapered leg, reminding me of a jogger-style silhouette that is more popular in female suits.
13. These leather Bermuda shorts remind me of male fashion due to their material. I see myself associating leather with more male attire.
14. This Dior chain belt reminds me of male attire because of the chain pattern; however, it accentuates the waist, reminding me more of female attire.
15. This white satin shirt is a staple in many female closets. The satin fabric is more associated with female fabrics, along with the bow detail around the neck. The collared shirt, however, reminds me of male dress shirts.
16. These cowboy boots are made of crocodile leather, which I associate with a more male material. However, cowboy boots are worn by all genders and can be a staple in anyone's closet.

17. I chose these layered necklaces because layered jewelry reminds me of a more female fashion concept. However, the silver metal, chain, and lock remind me more of male jewelry.
18. These gold dangle earrings give me remanences of female fashion because of the dangle from the hoop and the crystal material detail. However, I feel as though a male would wear this in one ear.
19. This makeup look is done on a male model. It is more typical of women to wear eyeliner; however, the structure and clean lines of this look can accentuate any outfit no matter the gender. The pop of color is more often associated with female makeup; however, to make this look more unisex, I would make the liner black.
20. A tuxedo jacket is mostly associated with male fashion. However, the tapered silhouette and the tweed fabric make this jacket appeal to all genders.
21. A necktie is more frequently associated with male fashion; however, brands like Hermes have popularized a woman's necktie, as seen in the photo clip.
22. Although stockings are more associated with female fashion, the distressed style of these stockings remind me more of male attire. The texture of the stockings make them a unisex accessory.
23. These sunglasses have a more manly silhouette due to the blocky, rectangular shape they have. However, the light brown color and gold details on the handle make them appealing to female consumers as well.
24. A beret is popular in both male and female fashion, especially in Europe. It can be dressed up or dressed down by all genders. The neutral color of accessories such as the beret make them more unisex.
25. I chose this watch because it is a staple worn by all genders. The silhouette is sleek, appealing to both styles. Furthermore, the dual-tone metals make the accessory popular with any consumer.
26. A romper is most often associated with being a female article of clothing. However, this all-black romper with a looser and blockier silhouette and structured fabric appeals to male audiences.
27. A vest is more commonly associated with male fashion and male tuxedos. However, the more fitted silhouette, flowy fabric, and ribbon details make it wearable in female fashion.
28. Colored contacts are a fun way to spruce up any outfit. No eye color is associated with a specific gender; however, all genders can play with their look by changing their eye color.
29. A long, slicked-back ponytail is associated with female fashion. However, the slicking back of the hair accentuates the cheekbones and lifts the face, accentuating more masculine facial features.

30. Black-and-white sneakers are a staple in any closet. The neutral colors along with the structured silhouette (with no featured heel) make the shoe unisex.

Our university's visual and performing arts department includes programs in theatre; art history; studio art; music; and film, television, and media arts. Fashion Forward is listed as a theatre course and is also cross-listed with art history. Roughly half the students enroll through each program listing. The class is an upper-level elective for theatre or art history majors and minors and is open to all students in the university as an arts elective.

While not strictly a theatre course, in terms of its content and focus, Fashion Forward serves the theatre program's commitment to inclusivity, formulated in 2021. Our statement reads:

> Theatre transports us into an infinite variety of lives and experiences, where we can deepen our understanding of what it means to be human. Theatre artists and scholars build empathy, celebrate diversity, examine our beliefs and practices, encourage global citizenship, and empower all people.

This statement was a guiding principle in the development of course material and structure.

Fashion Forward is also an approved social justice signature element course in our university's Magis Core curriculum. This curriculum, first implemented in Fall of 2021, "engages students to establish their own values and understanding of the world while emphasizing excellence in writing, critical reasoning, synthesis of solutions, communication, and an understanding of the 'why' and 'how' of associated human behaviors," according to the Fairfield University course catalogue. To earn the social justice designation, a course must "accomplish the learning outcomes through a focus on race, broadly construed, studied intersectionality with gender and class." Exactly as this course intended to do.

The course has sparked interest from faculty and students in several different programs, including peace and justice studies; anthropology; and women, gender, and sexuality studies. It may be cross-listed in some of these programs in future semesters. It is also a recommended course for business school students wishing to earn a minor in fashion marketing: Students are advised to take Fashion Forward before taking their six classes required for the minor in Florence, Italy. The study of fashion history is perhaps gaining value on campus more quickly than anticipated.

Preparing to teach Fashion Forward has fostered greater connections between myself and faculty in other areas of academic study at our university.

Figure 4.4 Slide from final student project: Fast Fashion and Social Justice
Source: Hailey Bruner, 2022

Since I began work on developing this course, I have been a guest lecturer in several classes, including a Black Lives Matter class (discussing the intersection of the Black Lives Matter movement with the blockbuster musical *Hamilton*) and a Latin class (giving an overview and demonstration of the Roman toga). Future collaborations with colleagues in English literature, studio art, and chemistry are in discussion for both guest lecture and team-teaching opportunities. I was also invited by the Belarmine Museum to give an online talk about the work of photographer Lalla Essaydi and to serve on a panel discussion the work of textile artist and sculptor Tamsen Williams's "The Dying Gaul." These professional collaborations have proved the theory that fashion history and costume design are, by their nature, interdisciplinary and rigorous subjects worthy of sharing with the greater campus community.

Looking Back

Fashion Forward was first offered during the tail end of the COVID-19 pandemic, which presented several logistical challenges. Most notably, the first time this course was offered, many museums were still virtual spaces, and campus safety protocols forbade off-campus field trips. This prevented us from visiting an in-person fashion exhibition, which would have been an exceedingly helpful touchstone in understanding the final project. Hopefully, this will not be an ongoing issue. However, we do have an on-campus museum and several galleries, so perhaps one work-around is to develop a sample exhibition on campus.

Student absenteeism, stress, and burnout also presented obstacles to learning. Flexible deadlines and constant communication with students eased this somewhat – I have found that students are far more eager to do the work for a professor who "sees" them than one who keeps their distance – but it is clear that the two years of the pandemic's disruption will have lasting consequences on student and teacher behavior and expectations.

I was concerned about potential pushback from students, as some parts of the country have spoken out against a "woke" agenda in academia. I made a point to stress that the content of and focus of the course was meant to provoke thought and provide opportunity for reflection and paths forward, not to shame or blame students for events or ideas of the past. I opened the class on the first day with a brief overview of Chris Muller's lecture, "The March of (Costume) History," in which he linked the teaching of costume history in Eurocentric chronological order to the 1420 procession in honor of Cosimo Di Medici. "This is how we've been doing things," I told them. I then followed up with the "Stuff" clip from the film *The Devil Wears Prada* (wherein high-powered fashion magazine editor Miranda Priestly berates her new assistant Andy for not grasping the complexities of the fashion system that permeate every so-called "choice" we make when we get dressed). "I'm no Miranda," I said, "but we might all be a little like Andy when it comes to global fashion history. There is so much we don't know, because someone else decided it wasn't important. Let's see what we can learn together." I was relieved that students felt safe and respected enough in the classroom to be vulnerable and open to learning.

Students responded very positively to the course, the content, and the class structure. Discussions were robust and thoughtful; students felt empowered to talk about their own experiences, their changing awareness of history, and their growing consciousness as part of the fashion system. This was a pleasant surprise. While they found some of the readings a challenge – something I need to address in the next rotation of this course – they felt the information gleaned from them was valuable and the in-class discussions to be a key part of their learning process. They also felt the assignments gave them creative and intellectual freedom.

The final piece of in-class, ungraded writing is a self-reflection journal prompt. Students respond to the following questions:

- ◆ What about this course surprised you? What challenged you? What confused you?
- ◆ What about this course will stick with you?

- How did/did this course change you as a student, a writer, a consumer of fashion, a citizen, or a human being?
- What will you use from this class to change the world?

They then share their responses with each other.

Most students state that the course was an eye-opener for them on many levels. "I never knew . . ." and "I hadn't realized . . ." are common themes. They confess to sometimes feeling uncomfortable as they reexamined previously held positions. They also express surprise at how fashion seems to impact almost every facet of human interaction. Some feel called to action, pledging to shop and dress in a more sustainable way. Some say they are working on developing a more personal sense of style, taking inspiration from the ideas discussed in class. Others express a desire to be more culturally aware in their future fashion choices. Many say they are much more observant and less judgmental when noticing how other people dress. And almost all express an interest in learning more about different people, places, and ways of expressing identity and community through fashion.

Students did find some of the content intellectually challenging, particularly readings from more scholarly sources. Additionally, while I thought the short assignments created a clear scaffold that could serve as a pathway for their final research projects, some students didn't see the connections until I pointed them out. ("Remember how we did this in that assignment last month? That's what you should do here, but more in depth!") So there is more work to be done.

Thinking Ahead

Potential areas to improve course content include:

- A mini-lesson on how to read "academic" texts and articles;
- Collaboration with art history faculty on museum exhibition how-tos;
- Making more explicit connections between the small scaffolding assignments and the final project; and
- Continuing to seek out new materials to share, new ideas to explore, new guest lecturers to invite, and new communities to include.

5

Global Dress History for Undergraduate General Education

Anastasia Goodwin

From the Beginning

The most essential goal for the course was to get students to understand that fashion is not a Western-only cultural idea but, rather, something fundamentally human. Linda Welters and Abby Lillethun in their book *Fashion: A Global History* explain the idea of "the fashion instinct" – the urge that exists in every human culture ever studied to adorn ourselves in some way. Therefore, in order to disrupt the narrative of fashion as a progression of Western silhouettes, students were called to explore the deep social currents that drive changes in dress anytime, anywhere. My second goal was to bring the physical aspect of dress and fashion – i.e., the textiles, construction practices, and finishing techniques – into the students' classroom experience. Contemporary Western culture largely treats items of dress as commodities, readily available and frequently disposable. In the absence of a museum or costume collection in close proximity, I brought into the room things that the students could see and touch so we wouldn't just talk about materials in the abstract but connect the conceptual to the physical. This allowed the class to keep its heritage as a course born out of theatre design (the dialogue between the conceptual and the physical is the essential modus operandi of our discipline); even more than that, it demonstrated that everything discussed in class, no matter how remote in terms of time or geography, does have a connection to the students' everyday lives. In other words, this stuff matters!

DOI: 10.4324/9781003278184-6

> School: Saint Mary's University of Minnesota
>
> Department: Fine and Performing Arts; Theatre Program
>
> Student Level/Description: General undergraduate audience; junior-level class
>
> Class Size: 5–20; first cohort: 6 students
>
> Hours/Week: 3 credit hours
>
> Format: In person; currently building an online section
>
> Text or Core Materials: Readings from books, academic articles, and contemporary news media as well as documentaries and instructor-generated lectures, field trip, and guest speaker presentations
>
> Types of Access Needed: All course materials, assignments, and student communication were hosted on the institutional learning management system (Canvas). Students were required to have a laptop, tablet, or any other device that allowed them to work with Canvas in class. Other Learning Technology Used: Google Suite programs, Padlet, Zoom (for guest speaker presentations).

Reasons to Adapt

A fundamental understanding of material/visual history is of utmost importance not only for future costume professionals but also for all directors, designers, and technicians of theatre. Performers and theorists also benefit greatly from this grounding. Even more broadly, basic material culture knowledge should be required of any liberal arts graduate because it is foundational to the development of an understanding of culture, place, identity, sociality, belonging, and aesthetic tendencies. Yet it is largely absent from the general history discourse at the undergraduate level. Students learn global and national history in the form of dates, names, and events; they learn theatre history in terms of literary and artistic movements; and those who learn art history through traditional courses also tend to focus more on the conceptual and thematic rather than the material tools or methods. What is missing from this view is the connection of history to humanity, to the everyday realities of people of all walks of life. The cultural and functional aspects of dress can be seen as a throughline in all human history – after all, we all get up and get dressed in some way every day. Studying the clothing habits of any particular culture can therefore be the easiest passage into how its members think or thought, what they deem(ed) important, and how they communicate(d) this, consciously and subconsciously, to others.

After teaching a compressed survey of Western fashions in my costume design class, I began working toward the goal of creating and teaching a separate course that would focus on dress history. When this process began, my thinking was still very much wrapped up in the idea of the timeline. After all, historical developments and events follow each other sequentially; certain ideas, technologies, and materials are only made possible by what came before. And yet, as we look at the events from the past with scholarly inquiry, we notice connections, patterns, and philosophical understandings of the world that rise and fall in popularity and prominence in what might be interpreted as a cyclical nature. I realized that I had come to rely on the timeline for context: Certain things happened in a certain culture, and there was a way they manifested in its people's appearances. However, linear time is not the only way to contextualize history. Furthermore, most undergraduate students do not come into my program with a solid base in global or even American history or geography. So, for example, telling students that something occurred during the 1790s in France would not automatically signal the revolution and complete restructuring of aristocratic society. However, contextualizing content along the lines of identity, power, privilege, and access to resources was something that students could easily and clearly grasp because these ideas are very present in their current worldviews. Letting go of the timeline was not easy; I struggled with the thought that without it, the class would become disorganized, that I would have no way to provide the academic rigor that is expected both by our discipline and by my students, and that content would just be a jumble of beautiful things. Three things that helped me come around and fully embrace teaching differently are: 1) Reminding myself that no one class is capable of containing, teaching, or presenting all of global dress history – the subject is simply too vast. Editing the content in a way that is disruptive of the notion of Western supremacy is, therefore, the paramount task; 2) in order to maintain the structure and organization of the content, my conceptual "signal posts" had to be strong, clearly observable, and present in the students' daily lives; and 3) teaching methodology had to shift away from the slide show/quiz format and allow for students' active engagement with the material as standard classroom practice. In other words, in order to change the what, the how had to change as well.

In order for my class to have maximum impact, I wanted to make sure it would be open and accessible to students of all majors and many possible professional and educational interests. This meant that the class covered broad topics rather than digging really deeply into any one specific detail of global dress and that looking at the interplay between the individual, the cultural, the industrial, and the political impacts of it was the core around which learning goals and objectives were created. The commodification of dress in contemporary society leaves many students with few ways to analyze their own roles in what it means to be a participant in global fashion. After all, most of them have come to expect garments that cost less than restaurant meals, and the labor that goes into any article of clothing from design to consumer is largely hidden and therefore easily ignored. Thus, my unstated (but hopefully obvious in retrospect) goal for the course was a focus on the humanity of the material. Within every topic we discussed, I made sure to bring into sharp focus the human factor. This lens allowed us not only to address the goal of dismantling the idea of Western supremacy in fashion but also to be inclusive of the overall goals of a liberal arts education. Though the course retained its roots in theatrical design mostly through teaching methodology, the humanistic framework made it accessible even to those students who had never taken a theatre, art, or fashion course. My tagline is "Do you get dressed in the morning? Then this class is for you!"

Course Objectives
- Recognize dress and fashion as a global human activity;
- Contemplate how ideas and materials of dress travel across the globe and over time and how these processes either support or subvert power structures and traditions within societies; and
- Wrestle with their own position as arbiters, creators, and curators of fashion and whether their consumption practices line up with or contradict their stated values.

Learning Outcomes
- Research methodology: Students learned to use a variety of image databases, as well as research databases. Students also learned the distinctions between academic and industry publications, as well as general online resources.
- Creating effective presentations: Students practiced a variety of ways to present their work digitally
- Basic sewing and home-dyeing skills: Our *shibori* project focused on these, and it made the students' responses to further references to labor and skill much deeper and more thoughtful. In other words, it provided important context, especially for those students who didn't usually work in the costume shops.
- Cultural literacy: Through readings, guest lectures, and discussions, students were able to become better equipped to talk about different traditions, cultures, and issues (both historical and modern day) in academically appropriate ways.

- Critical thinking and self-reflection: I put an emphasis on making students question why they find things attractive, appealing, or the opposite. I asked them to examine their emotional responses objectively – not to deny or judge them, but to explore where they were coming from. This allowed them to understand that many of our ideas of beauty are learned within the context of our culture, and therefore, no one way to express these ideas is "better" or "more correct". I see this as a step in dismantling the notion that Western supremacy is an inevitability.
- Empathy: I see this course as being focused on people. Elements of dress are expressions of our collective humanity. So, whether our topic was leather making, corsetry, or tattooing; whether we examined dress practices in Edo Japan or the "folk dress" of Scandinavian cultures, I always made sure to say, "A person made this. Someone's hands touched this. There are people out there in the world who stitched our contemporary T-shirts together". By switching students' perspective from clothing as commodity to seeing it as a product of human labor and skill many times over, I hope to build more ways in which they can become more connected to the community and the world around them.

Table 5.1 Syllabus Calendar

Date/Week/Module	Topics and Instructional Activities	Readings and Graded Assignments
Module 1: Introduction Week 1/2	What is this class? What is fashion? What is dress? What is history?	Personal Reflection 1
Module 2: Body Modifications Week 2	Impermanent modifications: Hair, makeup, body paint	Online discussion response
Week 3	Permanent modifications: Tattooing, scarification, body binding, implants	Research Project 1 Online discussion response

(*Continued*)

Table 5.1 Continued

Date/Week/Module	Topics and Instructional Activities	Readings and Graded Assignments
Module 3: Textiles Week 4	Non-woven and Woven textiles	Personal Reflection 2 Online discussion response
Week 5	Dye methods and hands-on project	In-class work Online discussion response
Week 6	Environmental and labor practices and impact of the textile and garment industries	Maker project Research Project 2 Online discussion response
SPRING BREAK		
Module 4: Silhouettes Week 7	Manipulating woven textiles: Cutting and draping	Final project proposal
Week 8	Manipulating the human form	Personal Reflection 3 Online discussion response
Week 9	Changing silhouette as a signifier of fashion	Research Project 3
Module 5 Cultural Exchanges Week 10	Trade routes in pre- and early colonial world	Online discussion response
Week 11	Effects of Western colonial expansion	Personal Reflection 4
Week 12	Dress as identity	Research Project 4 Online discussion response
Weeks 13–14	Review and synthesis of major ideas	Final project written components
FINAL EXAM	Presentation and in-class responses to final projects	Final project visual components

Source: Anastasia Goodwin, 2022

Table 5.2 Rubric for a "read the label" assignment. Students were asked to look at the label of their favorite garment and research both the manufacturing practices for the fibers listed and the labor practices in the garment's country of origin

Criteria	Ratings			Points
Photo of Garment	5 points Photo of garment and label included; all writing clearly visible	3 points Photos of low quality, label not properly shown	0 points No photo	5 points
Fiber Research	25 points All the components of the label are sufficiently addressed using the questions in the assignment description	13 points Some components missing or research incomplete	0 points Section missing entirely	25 points
Manufacturing Practices Research	25 points All questions pertaining to manufacturing and labor practices are sufficiently addressed	13 points Only some of the questions are addressed or answered incompletely	0 points Section missing entirely	25 points
Personal Statement	20 points An honest effort made to address the way your research findings affect your relationship with the garment	10 points Response too brief and surface level; shows little effort to address self-reflective questions	0 points Section missing entirely	20 points
Total Points: 75				

Source: Anastasia Goodwin, 2022

Process in Creating the Course

My dissatisfaction with previous teaching methods came to light during a course I took in online instructor certification from my institution. Pre-2020, I probably would not ever have considered teaching theatre online; however, in the current world, denying the fact that at some point many of us will be teaching at least a portion of our current loads online would be similar to denying electric light 150 years ago. I decided to obtain the certification with the thought that if I'm going to be teaching online, I might as well figure out how to do it well. What I discovered was that a) teaching at the college level is one of the only jobs out there in which you are evaluated on your performance before anyone actually shows you how to do it, and b) theatre is no different than any other academic discipline, except for education itself – one's proficiency in the subject matter is always assumed to make them a competent educator – and I believe we can all point to examples of this assumption being incorrect in a number of cases. This certification course was the first time I was taught how to teach, and it was quite eye opening.

One of my biggest takeaways was the realization of the true importance of my learning objectives. This point was reiterated when I took the costume history syllabus workshop led by Chloe Chapin, following the larger collective online conference Re-Dressing the Narrative, Part 2, organized by Chapin and Christianne Myers of the American Theatrical Costumer Association (ATCA). The process of designing or restructuring any course has to begin with the following questions: What is the overall purpose of this course? What do I want students to know when they leave? In what way do I want them to change? Also important to consider were my goals as an educator: How did I want to grow? What did I want to get better at? What were my strengths as an artist, practitioner, and mentor that I was most capable of and keen on sharing?

Arriving at the answers to these questions definitely took time and self-reflection. I thought about all the wonderful teachers and mentors in my life, as well as any classes I could remember, even from my youth, that felt like the lessons stuck. Harriet Schwartz, in her wonderful book *Connected Teaching*, talks about teaching being one of the most self-reflective endeavors one can undertake, and that is no overstatement. After all this thinking, jotting down, and first drafting, I came out knowing that I wanted students to know that dress is a phenomenon of human self-expression free of ownership by any one culture, however dominant; I wanted them to see that history is a collection of stories about factual events (rather than the events themselves), and none are entirely free of biases that should be acknowledged and examined to understand nuanced concepts and ideas; and I wanted to train them in research methods that would help them find the information they needed when they needed it, as opposed to making them memorize terminology or dates.

What followed was a significant foray into education literature pertaining to learning science and theories and teaching methods and philosophical explorations of how teaching methods do or do not relate to disciplinary content and practice. While fulfilling and exciting in its own right, this amount of research is certainly not necessary for the task at hand. But it helped me wrap my mind around the idea of costume history and dress theory as dynamic rather than static subjects. In this view, in order to create a significant learning experience for my students, my goal was to design projects and activities that would allow them to explore interesting questions and to follow their own ideas of what was worthy of inquiry, rather than maniacally learning all the global costume history facts and terminology to create thousands more slides.

> **Quick In-class Activity**
>
> Students work in pairs or small groups on a quick research prompt. It can be related to global dress history ("What was the primary textile used in ____ region in _____ time?" in which the blanks are different for each student group) or contemporary issues ("What is a certified B corporation in relation to fashion?"). One member of the group is typically tasked with putting the results into the class PowerPoint, which we then view as a group. I had several of those throughout the class, making sure the recorders and presenters weren't always the same students.

Once I chose my conceptual signposts, which became my modules for the course, each encompassing three to four weeks of study, I worked on figuring out how the students could best show their engagement with, understanding of, and proficiency at these concepts. In my instruction, I focused on presenting a topic as a set of questions and gave students a series of examples of how they might go about conducting research to answer them. They were then given choices on the specifics of content and the parameters of how to conduct their inquiry. This approach meant I had to contend with the possibility of students exploring content that I myself hadn't encountered before. I found it was still very possible to evaluate students' work and advise them on improvement by basing assessment on their methods, sources, and thought processes. The idea of teaching unfamiliar content can be daunting, but the plain and simple truth is that our students don't have time for us to acquire expertise in every possible iteration of global dress. Equally problematic become the queries such as "I am thinking of adding some non-Western content to my class. What should I add: China? Korea? Central Africa?" because, inevitably, the question from the students would be "Why are we studying A instead of B?" which is really the question "What set of criteria did the instructor use to determine one culture/time period more worthy of inclusion than the other?" I chose instead to focus the class on concepts present in all dress systems and then allowed students to choose the specifics they felt were close to their own identities, putting into practice the fundamental principle of anti-colonial thinking: That no one dress culture is "better" or "more worthy of study" than any other.

To summarize, my process looked something like this. As in any design process, these steps didn't always happen in a linear way, and there was some back-and-forth adjustment and refinement of all syllabi, materials, and readings.

- Created learning objectives based on what I would like the students to be able to do;
- Figured out the structure for my course, as well as what kind of assignments would be best suited to the learning objectives;
- Asked myself which instruction methods would be the most conducive to the kind of thinking I would like my students to engage in;
- Devised a final project that required students to put together all the skills they learned with a personal interest;
- Created the course calendar based on weeks of instruction and chose my readings, videos, and other content-bearing materials, selecting more than I knew we could get through for additional flexibility;
- Reached out to any outside parties I involved in my course: Instruction librarian, local museum, guest speaker, the maker space; and
- Refined my syllabus, assignment sheets, and rubrics. The last two continued to be adjusted throughout the class as I got more familiar with this group of students and this still-new format.

One Brief Bit of Advice

Include a practical project for which students have to create something with their hands. Depending on what's possible in terms of budget, material costs, and facilities, as well as your and their comfort level with various tools and techniques, this could be weaving, dyeing, draping, embroidery or embellishment, or any number of things. The project doesn't need to be

> extensive – 1 or 2 classes or about 3 class hours should be enough, but it needs to be connected to the theoretical concepts learned in class. I encourage you to do this sooner in the semester rather than later because the students will learn to understand and appreciate the labor and skill of the original makers in a way that is much more immediate and visceral than, say, just learning from a lecture, video, or reading. This emotional connection, in turn, will lead to more authentic inquiry for the rest of the class.

Broader Connections

Ours is a Bachelor of Arts in theatre undergraduate program at a small, private Catholic university. Though we offer a robust production experience, the program has broad liberal arts goals within the larger framework of Lasallian education, with emphasis on service, social justice, human dignity, and community building. There are four tracks within the major (design/technology, musical theatre, acting/directing, and theatre studies), each with slightly different requirements in course and production work, all arranged around a core that includes courses in analysis, history, and the basics of every aspect of production work. We do not require our designer/technicians to audition; however, all majors receive a scholarship that requires production participation in some way. Since our programmatic goals include cultural competency, critical thinking, research proficiency, and aesthetic sensibility, the course on global dress history was a very obvious fit. Students learned about cultures outside their own, learned research methods for visual disciplines, experienced many forms of beauty, and had plenty of ways to discuss, argue, and think through concepts like beauty ideals, cultural expectations, ways to express identity, and the connections between the material and the conceptual.

Thinking Back on the Process

Overall, I enjoyed almost everything about this class, from the initial idea to the day of turning in my final grades. I think that, in many ways, this was the first time I felt that I was creating something new and my own, as opposed to copying my teachers. Now, I feel very lucky to say that all who taught me have been wonderful, amazing educators and are a continuing source of inspiration. But one of the big reasons for this is the fact that now, in retrospect, I can see that they, too, never settled for the familiar. They challenged their students, as well as themselves, and they were never afraid to make me dig deeper, ask one more why, find one more source. So I feel that with this class, I was finally able to take the gifts they gave me and create something that is necessary for this moment right now.

All this is not to say that I think the class was perfect. I took a little bit of a kitchen-sink approach with my instruction methods, so we had it all: Readings, films, several types of discussions, short in-class lectures, all kinds of research projects, several bits of flashy instructional tech, and a couple of papers for good measure. And though students, overall, enjoyed the class and learned a lot, in the future, I definitely plan on focusing my approach to reduce the cognitive load by creating a sense of depth in the class, which is inherently marked by so much breadth. The methods I do plan on keeping are:

- In-class discussions, with questions that students can prepare ahead of time;
- In-class research projects;
- Well-made and credible documentaries to replace the majority of lectures; and
- Guest speakers and field trips.

In addition, I would like to add more hands-on projects and to tie research assignments to those projects. I would also make the students' weekly processes (i.e., the kinds of preparation they need to do) more consistent, in order to reduce the cognitive load for things that are less consequential.

The universal applicability of a global dress history course in an undergraduate liberal arts institution is something I hope more educators will take advantage of. As my current institution is trying to move toward becoming a pre-med and nursing hub, there is a demand in the relatively new field of health humanities, and I fully intend to market this course for a program such as that. After all, clothing and items of dress are a fundamental part of the issues of identity and humanity and answer questions about how we move through every stage of our lives and deaths. The students in programs that are not theatre bring perspectives into classrooms that are so diverse, so inspiring, and so meaningful that the teaching experience itself becomes a source of great joy. These students – the scientists, the business majors, the writers, the athletes – contrary to what some may say, really do want to hear what we have to say. They are just as hungry for understanding the thing so fundamental to our work – how our personhood is expressed through what we wear – as any costume student I have ever met. In turn, our experiences, our approaches, and our methods are so, so valuable to them. And if we costumers are to move out of theatre basements and from the fringes of academia to take our rightful place among the rest of the disciplines, they are definitely a big part of getting us there.

6

Historic Costume and Décor Utilizing a People- and Place-Based Curriculum

Maile Speetjens and Michelle Bisbee

School: University of Hawai'i at Mānoa

Department: Department of Theatre and Dance, College of Arts, Languages, and Letters

Course Title: Historic Costume and Décor

Major/General Education/Level: Graduate course, built with MFA candidates and advanced undergraduate students in mind. This course has been taken by undergraduate students in fashion design and merchandising, women's studies, and theatre. Graduate students have been designers, actors interested in period styles, and directors.

Usual Class Size: Seminar, approximately 7–10

Class Format: Synchronous, in person (first 2 weeks conducted online due to COVID-19)

Texts or Materials Required:

Mida, Ingrid and Kim, Alexandra. *The Dress Detective: A Practical Guide to Object-Based Research in Fashion*, Bloomsbury Collections, 2022.

Piesik, Sandra, ed. *Habitat: Vernacular Architecture for a Changing Planet*, Abrams, 2017.

Postrel, Virginia. *The Fabric of Civilization: How Textiles Made the World*, First ed., Basic Books, Hachette Book Group, 2020.

> Types of Access Needed: This class was centered around place-based learning, taking advantage of the physical spaces and experiential learning environment found in Hawai'i, including archival research. Access to the internet and the university library was required.
>
> Range of Material: This was the only class of its kind offered by the department and needed to cover costume, architecture, and decor over the course of one semester.

Course Objectives
- Re-centering Hawai'i as a unique and indigenous place with a diverse and complex history, expressed in this class through material culture;
- Utilizing ethical and specific research methodologies for the visual realm;
- Using embodied knowledge and making as forms of research;
- Utilizing frameworks modified from the fields of multicultural curriculum studies, material culture studies (specifically object analysis), and decolonial writers of the Pacific/Oceania region;
- Ensuring that the people are not lost in the history; and
- Creating a community of learners encouraging, challenging, and supporting each other.

Learning Outcomes
- Utilize ethical and specific research methodologies for the visual realm as it pertains to performance design;
- Tailor research to the specifics of a particular creative project, understanding that styles are contextual and dependent on time/place/economic status/culture/social status/a myriad of other contextual considerations;
- Describe contextual motivation of visual/material culture changes over time and their relation to visual style shifts;
- Understand how costume, adornment, décor, architecture, and objects of everyday life relate to each other in a given specific cultural context;
- Visually recognize, compare, and contrast a variety of visual styles throughout the world and throughout history; and
- Explore the physical techniques involved in the creation of material objects in order to glean a deeper understanding of visual styles and makers through embodied knowledge.

As departmentally dictated, classes met for 1 hour and 15 minutes twice per week over the course of 16 weeks, with a final exam period. Students were assigned substantial reading, listening (podcasts), and viewing assignments to be conducted at home in preparation for in-class discussions, short presentations, and activities. Additionally, field trips were organized at the very beginning of the semester in order to accommodate student schedules and transportation and occurred on the weekends as a way of allowing students to spend more time at the locations if desired. Scaffolding occurred in the following manner:

Table 6.1 Module Breakdown

Weeks 1–2	Weeks 4–12	Weeks 13–16
Introduction to Slow Looking and Object Analysis	Exploration of Material Culture (organized by materials, construction, and finishing)	Synthesis: Objects and . . . (gender, status, intercultural exchange, colonialism, trade, spiritualism, technology, etc.)

Source: Maile Speetjens, 2022

Table 6.2 Syllabus Calendar

Week	Day	Class Subject	Homework/Reading
1	M	Introduction to research methodologies, styles and resources, slow-looking exercise, objects that matter	
	W	Introduction to research methodologies, styles, and resources	Week 1 Journal Entry due
2	M	MLK Jr. Day	MLK Jr. Day
	W	Intro to material culture studies, in-class activity (research observation mini project)	Week 2 Journal Entry due

(*Continued*)

Table 6.2 Continued

Week	Day	Class Subject	Homework/Reading
3	M	Research observation mini project – present findings and discuss with class	Week 3 Journal Entry due
	W	Materials: Fibers, fabrics, dyestuffs	Object unveiling due
4	M	Materials: In class activity	Week 4 Journal Entry due **come prepared to possibly get dirty
	W	Finish in-class activity Materials: Décor, architecture	
	S	Visit Bishop Museum	
5	M	Field trip decompression and discussion Materials: Décor and architecture (continued)	Week 5 Journal Entry due Field Trip Reflection due
	W	Field trip (possible day off in observation)	
6	M	Construction: Garments construction	Week 6 Journal Entry due
	W	Construction: In-class activity (adornment)	
7	M	Presidents' Day	Presidents' Day
	W	Construction: Décor, architecture	Week 7 Journal Entry due
8	M	Construction: Maker's time	Week 8 Journal Entry due **come prepared to possibly get dirty
	W	Finishing: Adornment	
9	M	Finishing: Décor, architecture	Week 9 Journal Entry due
	W	Finishing: Finishing (in-class activity)	Objects in Context draft due 8 (schedule a time to meet outside of class) **come prepared to possibly get dirty

Week	Day	Class Subject	Homework/Reading
	M	Spring Break	Spring Break
	W	Spring Break	Spring Break
10	M	20th-century research interview presentations	Week 10 Journal Entry due 20th-Century Research Interview Project due
	W	20th-century research interview presentations	
	S	Field trip: Japanese tea ceremony	
11	M	Cohesion in costume and décor (objects in context and in conversation)	Week 11 Journal Entry due
	W	Field trip (possible day off in observation) This one still needs confirmation	
12	M	Synthesis: Case study	Week 12 Journal Entry due Field Trip Reflection due
	W	Synthesis: Case study	
13	M	Objects in context: Objects and gender	Week 13 Journal Entry due
	W	Objects in context: Objects and status	
14	M	Objects in context: Objects and spirituality	Objects in Context draft due Week 14 Journal Entry due
	W	Objects in context: Objects and technology	
15	M	Objects in context: Objects and age	Week 15 Journal Entry due
	W	Objects in context: Objects and material culture exchange	

(*Continued*)

Table 6.2 Continued

Week	Day	Class Subject	Homework/Reading
	S	Field trip to ʻIolani Palace	
16	M	Debrief field trip, general class reflection	Week 16 Journal Entry due Field Trip Reflection due
	W	Field trip (possible day off in observation)	
Final Period	F	7:30–9:30 a.m.	Final Object in Context presentation

Source: Maile Speetjens and Michelle Bisbee, 2022

Thematic elements are tied together by content delivery type – namely, the embodied experience as a means of deepening connection to content through experiential learning – and each module culminated in a field trip or in-class activity related to the topical content.

Building a Shared Vocabulary

Students were introduced to the object analysis method early on in the semester through the assigned text *The Dress Detective*. This framework allowed students to break down objects (and eventually aesthetic choices) into manageable sections that allowed for deeper exploration. The class also began with a slow-looking exercise as a way of centering the idea that deep, slow looking can reveal details, complications, dissonance, and areas for further exploration.

Connections Across the Curriculum

The University of Hawaiʻi at Mānoa and the entire UH system have made a commitment to creating a "Native Hawaiian Place of Learning." The university outlines 3 pathways towards this goal utilizing this imagery (https://manoa.hawaii.edu/nhpol/).

This endeavor is most clearly expressed in the department of theatre and dance through the departmental action plan. The four directives of this plan

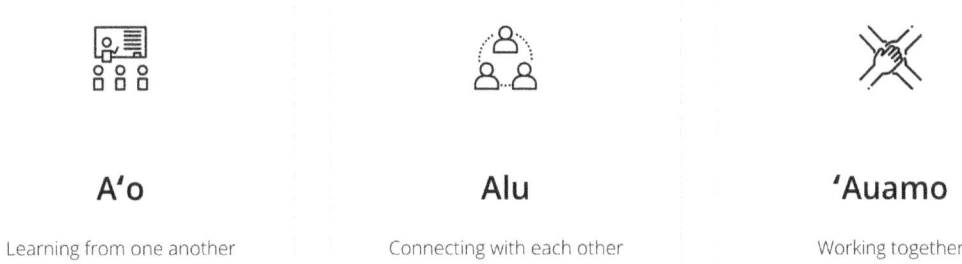

Figure 6.1 The University of Hawai'i logo for the 3 pathways to creating a Native Hawaiian Place of Learning

are outlined as "Centering Hawaiian Culture," "Diversifying Our Department Beyond a Western Focus," "Inviting Artists, Scholars, and Students of Color Into Our Department," and "Working for Inclusiveness," including the following statements: "The discussion on settler colonialism and the illegal occupation of Hawai'i Pae 'Āina [Archipelago] by the United States" and diversifying "existing courses with regard to reading assignments, assigned roles, discussion topics, and methodologies/techniques, etc." (https://manoa.hawaii.edu/liveonstage/tdap/).

Assessment components were generated with the intent of providing a variety of ways to respond to material and generate ideas, from weekly low-pressure class journal assignments to a cumulative Objects in Context project, encompassing a formal object analysis process, contextualizing paper, and the object being depicted in applicable theatrical settings.

Cumulative Class Portfolio/Journal

- ◆ Each week, students were assigned a prompt to respond to in a collaborative slide deck known as the class journal. Students worked together on one large, full-class collaborative journal and frequently discussed responses and findings in class.

Synthesis Day Discussion Leader

- ◆ Each student was responsible for coordinating a day of class to discuss their chosen topic, as well as contributing an article for the class to read that related to their topic. Examples of topics were objects and technology, objects and gender, objects and status, etc.

Field Trip Reflections

- Students reflected on their 3 major field trip experiences in writing and in class discussions, with question prompts such as "What were your expectations going into this place?" "What surprised you about the experience?" and "What further avenues of research did this experience call for?"

20th-Century Research Interview Project and Presentation

- Students conducted interviews with someone about their experience with material culture/architecture in their youth. They utilized these interviews as a way to pursue visual research into a specific time and place. This research was then juxtaposed against what "mainstream" perceptions of the era were.

Object Analysis Project

- This culminating project encompassed three components and was a major project throughout the semester. Students chose an object to focus on as a starting point, and

    1) analyzed the material, construction, and finishings of their chosen object through a formal object analysis process;
    2) researched and composed a paper about their object in a cultural context; and
    3) created a sense of the broader visual and societal context of the world that this object would exist in for theatrical purposes through curated visual research.

Initial Development of the Course Redesign Process

The first time in recent history that any type of period styles class was taught at the University of Hawaiʻi, Mānoa was in the spring of 2020. This new class was, at the time, developed with the mindset of trying to cover as much material as possible in the realms of dress, architecture, and objects of everyday life in a single semester. The format consisted primarily of lectures (one dress, one architecture and décor each week), outlining changes that occurred in these fields throughout the march of time. Discussions of how these elements related to larger societal factors and trends did arise, but deep discussion was thwarted by the need to "move on," lest the class fall behind the scheduled timeline. While the class was generally well received by students at the time, it was obvious by the end of the class (and the beginning of the COVID-19 pandemic) that the pace was untenable, the retention rate of students needed improving, and major elements of the global visual landscape were either being glossed over or left out completely. It was time to embark on a journey of change.

Teaching, learning, and designing at the University of Hawai'i, Mānoa are, as is true in many institutions, unique experiences. UHM is one of the most diverse and geographically isolated institutions in the world, and its department of theatre and dance offers programming in Hana Keaka (Hawaiian theatre) and traditional Asian theatre forms ranging from Kabuki to Xiqu to Wayang Listrik (and others), as well as theatre for young audiences and productions in the Euro-American theatrical tradition. Because of the diversity of both the student body and departmental offerings, it was abundantly clear at the onset of developing this course that creating a "traditional" historic costume and décor class would not serve the students or the department as a whole.

Initial questions of relative lecture-to-screen time became apparent at early planning meetings. While about half of the older iteration of this course involved non-Western styles, discussions spiraled into brow-furrowing exclamations ranging from "Is it even possible to teach *all* the 19th century variations in just 2 weeks?" to "Why are we spending 2 *whole* weeks on 100 years of the European wealthy aesthetic and *half* that time to cover all the dress practices in Japan . . . forever?" These discussions, while consternation inducing, allowed for a boiling-point moment. Clearly, neither a class nor a person can cover everything from everywhere, from the beginning of time. The class would need to be expanded out towards infinity, and there was never any way that a person teaching this class could specialize in this incredible breadth of knowledge without slighting one culture/time/place or another. Another major component in reassessing this course was the fact that the class needed to cover costume, architecture, and décor, all in a single semester, adding to the ultimate conclusion that the course needed to be rethought.

Additionally, it became increasingly obvious that many of the textbooks that have long been touted as the "be all and end all" of dress history had a decidedly specific lens: Namely, that the Eurocentric, wealthy silhouette was the touchstone and center around which to build and compare all other dress practices. Hawai'i, with its rich, complex, and multicultural visual history was rarely (if ever) mentioned in these texts and, if it was, was described through a highly problematic and exoticized lens. This proved to be true of other cultures as well, creating an obvious dissonance between the students in the class, their histories, and the formalized version of history portrayed in these texts. Rather than utilizing the massive slide shows featuring the wealthy white sector of what has been determined to be "fashion," students needed to see their lived experiences and histories present in the class, as well as to examine and interrogate the subject matter at hand.

It became apparent that the course would need to be composed instead primarily of articles, chapters, podcasts, and viewings rather than a single guiding textbook. It also became apparent through weekly research assignments in the class that contemporary 21st-century classrooms and learners have a vastly different set of research tools available at their fingertips than previous generations of learners had. At this point in time, there are reliable website compendiums, museum archives, digital library collections, and so much more available in any place and at any time. But with this incredible quantity of data, the pedagogical issue then became that students did not clearly understand the process of vetting and critically analyzing these sources. Thus, another major learning objective of the new iteration of this course was focusing on contemporary research methodologies for the world of design.

New Adaptations: Getting Out of Line

Due to the problems with the traditional mode of teaching Historic Costume and Décor, we determined to reconceptualize the course. Fortunately, the rotation of classes departmentally allowed for a good span of time in order to conduct this work. (This course is taught every other year.) In building this new course, learning objectives became clear. Above all, however, the driving thought behind this course centered around ensuring that the class was a living, breathing experience that centered people and place in history and material culture.

Rather than focusing on the lecture format, lessons centered around experiential learning and action. Assigned readings, viewings, listenings, and short in-class lectures were paired with in-class hands-on experiments, guest speakers, and field trips as a method of reinforcement and deeper engagement through the experiential learning.

Structurally, the course broke linear chronological conventions, and prioritized making and makers through the following modules:

- Materials: What do we use to make our dress, architecture, décor?
- Construction: How do we put together our dress, architecture, décor?
- Finishing: In what ways do we decorate our dress, architecture, décor?
- Synthesis: How do these elements relate to the broader social picture, both culturally and onstage?

In creating modules centered around material culture, it became much easier to break the perceived "linear narrative" of dress history and expand outward in unanticipated ways. While creating content supporting these modules, the structure also allowed for the flexibility to make connections (and contrasts) between time and cultures without necessarily centering or favoring a specific time or place. An additional advantage to this altered structure was that it allowed for numerous connections to be made in myriad ways between costume, architecture, and décor. Finally, this object-centered approach made space for students to connect with objects and history through hands-on, maker-centered projects.

By centering objects and makers, students had the opportunity to speak with specialists and guest lecturers in their field, including having the experience of making alongside practitioners. In keeping with the departmental action plan's directive to center Hawai'i in course and production work, invited guest artists were Kānaka Maoli practitioners, including Kumu Lauhala and Keoua Nilsen (Kumu Lauala) for weaving and Mele Kahalepuna Chun (Kumu Hulu) for Hawaiian featherwork practices. Bringing in these practitioners allowed students to work alongside experts in their craft, as well as to listen to their shared experiences. The informality of working with one's hands and gathering around to listen to a teacher instruct, correct, tell stories, and answer questions allows for experiential learning, one of the most valuable modes of learning possible. This type of learning is also deeply embedded in theatrical practices, allowing theatre students to draw on approaches they are already familiar with, even if the particular content was not familiar.

Field trips were also scheduled throughout the semester. These field trips allowed students to contextualize in-class lectures, discussions, and readings. Students remarked on the excitement they felt about actually attending a physical space, both learning about history in general and becoming more aware of their surroundings. One particular field trip involved visiting an authentic Japanese teahouse (incidentally, located on the campus of UHM). Rather than just touring the teahouse, however, students participated in a tea ceremony demonstration, allowing them to encounter the sensory experience of actually inhabiting a teahouse after viewing ground plans, images, and interpretation through a short in-class lecture. (Incidentally, one of the very few inauthentic aspects of this experience was the dress of the demonstrators. Rather than yukata or kimono with obi, these demonstrators wore what they referred to as "Kimumu": A fusion piece made of Hawaiian-print cottons with an imbedded obi, pockets, a crossed-over neckline, and a straight-cut skirt. Essentially, this garment was created to mimic the functionality of the kimono in the tea process while being patterned and built in a way that most closely resembles the slim-cut Hawaiian dresses found in the 1960s and 1990s. Needless to say, this garment sparked a lively discussion over fusion, cultural authenticity, and the history of "Hawaiian-print" fabric in the next class.)

Many of the projects and activities in class involved detail-oriented explorations of specific objects or techniques. One large project that spanned the entire semester involved taking a very deep dive into a specific object, beginning with a formal object analysis as outlined in *The Dress Detective*, composing a paper about the societal significance of said object in the broader context, and culminating in the exploration of this object in the theatrical context through a creative project. Choosing to allow time for deep dives into specific items, techniques, and processes encouraged students to connect this type of in-depth research to the broader scale of designing for a show, illustrating the importance of in-depth research practices and the discoveries that can be gleaned from them.

An additional action-oriented assessment component of this course focused on the "synthesis" section of the course structure. After stepping through the previously mentioned modules, students were then asked to lead a class discussion day on the relationship between material culture and a number of predetermined topics such as technology, spirituality, colonization, status, etc. Each student chose their discussion topic and was asked to provide an article for the class to read, in addition to an article each from dress history and architecture/décor history (chosen by the professors). Students were invited to lead the class in whatever way they felt would be most effective in discussing the topic and were given some examples of class format as a starting point. As this was graduate-level class, the inclusion of pedagogical experimentation at the student level gave learners the opportunity for self-reflection and metacognition, as well as functional practice preparing for teaching coursework in a mode that did not require the lecture format. Students deftly discovered articles that were new to most of the class, and it was fascinating to observe student connections to the materials and prompts.

One of the major challenges of teaching in this style, however, was the continued need to find ways to contextualize this non-linear approach in a timeline so that students could make connections across geographic regions and, practically, have an understanding of where to start their research for a theatrical piece. There are, after all, complications to breaking out of the linear narrative!

Rather than drawing a line of time from "the beginning" through to "now", however, visual histories became more akin to the lifelong pursuit of filling in the pieces of a 3D puzzle that will never actually be complete; stress was put on the fact that it is impossible to know everything, but the key is to know where to start looking to fill in the part of the puzzle that needs to be clear in order for the project at hand to be developed. Pedagogically, time was treated as one of the factors to consider in research, alongside issues like status, gender, colonization, and others. Focus was also placed on ensuring that those linear connections were made with statements like "Meanwhile, at the same time in ___, quite the opposite (or quite the same) was occurring."

It was extremely valuable to be honest with students when discussing the style of this course. We started by acknowledging that the course was experimental in nature and that adjustments might be made throughout the course as feedback occurred. Naming the experimental nature of this course not only appeared to encourage feedback from students, but, from a teaching standpoint, it also gave the class freedom to feel more like a community of learners right from the outset of the course.

Sample Project

Fibers and Dyestuffs

This unit began with an in-class discussion and lecture on fibers, dyestuffs, and their relationship to societal elements such as politics, trade, class, technology, and indigeneity, each framed in the context of utilizing the material as a physical metaphor for (or perhaps even literal) manifestation of a societal element. (See Figure 6.2)

Examples of these framings include the following:

- ◆ Students learned about the Spanish colonization of Central American and their subsequent immense wealth (built on the backs and to the detriment of the native peoples) due in large part to the "discovery" (read: Appropriation) of the Nocheztli, tiny cactus bugs subsequently deemed cochineal;

Figure 6.2 Student and faculty member Maile Speetjens work over a pot of natural dyestuffs
Source: Michelle Bisbee, 2022

- Indigo was presented as a dye of some ubiquity, demonstrating technological chemical advances across many cultures through the use of alkaline baths and binding processes; and
- Finally, Hawaiian dyestuffs were introduced through the lens of sustainability, indigeneity, and the sacred, utilizing 'olena (Hawaiian turmeric) as a demonstration of high-value dye and color within the Hawaiian cultural sphere.

As a means of hands-on, embodied reinforcement of ideas, students then spent the next class period actually using these 3 exemplar dyes to alter the color of prepared fabrics. While students moved through stations of cochineal (complete with unprocessed bugs), 'olena, and indigo, discussions of the time and energy required to produce not just the dyestuffs but the fibers and woven fabrics being dyed emphasized the notion that clothing was an item of very high value prior to the rise of industrialization, the deeper understanding of which came in handy as the shifting "fashionable" European silhouette of the 19th/20th centuries and its relationship to fabric waste was discussed

Historic Costume and Décor ◆ 97

Figure 6.3 Students and faculty members work over several pots of natural dyestuff

Source: Michelle Bisbee, 2022

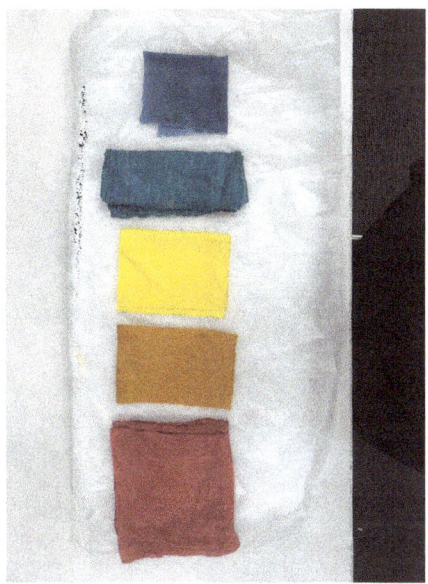

Figure 6.4 Sample colors produced from natural dye project

Source: Maile Speetjens, 2022

in the Construction module of this course. Students remarked that this understanding of the time and money that went into clothing production would factor into their costume design choices when depicting an earlier period.

Sample Activity 2

Construction Module Hands-On Activity

Lauhala Weaving with Kumu Keoua Nilsen

As an embodied (and Hawaiian-centered) introduction to the process of weaving, a Lauhala (Indigenous Hawaiian pandanus plant) weaving workshop was organized during class. Kumu Lauhala Keoua Nilsen visited the class and led a workshop on the basics of the process. While students worked with their hands, Kumu told stories of his lineage, answered questions about the cultural and historical context of the weaving process in Hawai'i, and reminded students of the contemporary relevance of this practice, showing images of a recent collaboration he did with a major global

Figure 6.5 Students work around a table learning Lauhala weaving techniques

Source: Michelle Bisbee, 2022

Historic Costume and Décor ◆ 99

Figure 6.6 Students and faculty put their hands together in the center of the circle to show their Lauhala woven bracelets

designer label. Students laughed, asked questions enthusiastically, and left wanting to learn more.

> Our cultures, contrary to the simplistic interpretation of our romantics, were changing even in pre-papalagi times. . . . No culture is ever static and can be preserved (a favourite word with our colonisers and romantic elite brethren) like a stuffed gorilla in a museum.
>
> Albert Wendt, *Towards a New Oceania*

Sample Activity 3

Weekly Collaborative Journal Prompts

Example: This week's prompt was "Choose a time/place and find an example of dress as expressed through status dynamics."

(*Note student and faculty comments on the slide, as well as additional slides with wildly different subject matter along the left-hand side.)

This necessary change to both the content and curricular approach to this class was spurred by observations of the student body that needed to be served by this class. A diverse body of 21st-century learners who had been learning online for years were no longer responding to in-person lectures

Figure 6.7 Image of a slide created by a student for class discussion for the weekly collaborative journal prompt

presented in a tidy, overly simplified, and Eurocentric causal chain of events. It was clear that this narrative was not just inaccurate and inauthentic in its simplification but was also harmful to the histories and lived experiences of the students entering this classroom. As a final driving reason for this change, the productions and workshops that UH Mānoa's student body was engaging with at the production season level were not reflected in this class, thus creating a disconnect between the traditional classroom sphere and the embodied lab experience within the department itself. It became clear that in order to serve my personal empathy-centered teaching philosophy, this class needed to change fundamentally.

Perhaps the most encouraging aspect of this work (aside from being a truly joyful class to teach and prepare for) has been the student response. During the course, students were clearly connecting with the material in their broader experiences. In addition to in-class discussions around the efficacy (or ineffectiveness) of the coursework and structure, it was clear through hallway discussions and informal emails that students were connecting the material in class to their daily lives. One student actually started uploading photos of local plants that could be used as dye to the class collaborative drive on their walks around campus. One particularly enthusiastic and generous (anonymous) student evaluation responded to the question "What were your expectations entering this course? Did they change over the course of the semester and, if so, how?" by responding as follows:

> Initially I thought it would be a generic history class, lots of reading, sit and listen to an hour+ long lecture over what we discussed. That

quickly changed and it was much more interesting than your run of the mill history class! Maile and Michelle have redefined how theatre practitioners learn, think about, and apply worldly techniques into our work as designers, [a]long with bringing in big life topics like how gender, spirituality, and material culture play into theatre.

Additionally, reverberations of this change in approach have made themselves evident in other course- and production work throughout the department. Students are more critical of resources, taking time to track down origins of interesting (and perhaps suspect) images found on the internet. Students are also more ready to acknowledge where more research is needed during early design meetings, rather than attempting a topical approach to complex visual scenarios.

Finally, and perhaps most importantly, students are making critical, ethically minded, and intentional choices about the visual world they are creating onstage and the potentially confusing or harmful ramifications of those decisions.

Because this class is offered infrequently (once every 4 semesters), the course had ample time to be developed, tweaked, and reassessed. With that in mind, however, this class is by no means "finished" or "perfect," and there were absolutely projects, areas of inquiry, and feedback that were unexpected once students were involved. Thus, this class by necessity is iterative, ever changing and morphing to meet, support, and challenge future students. Students indicated a desire for future iterations of this course to have deeper practice connecting research methodologies discussed in class and the practical application of working on research for a production.

7

An Abridged Clothing History in Four Construction Techniques

Lena Sands

School: Los Angeles Mission College, Verdugo Hills High School, Los Angeles County High School of the Arts

Department: Theatre (LAMC)/Visual Arts (LACHSA)

Level: Introductory Collegiate/Secondary Education

Class Size: 15–25 students

Class Format: In person

Usual Student Emphasis: Interested in theatre or fashion design

Texts Required: Selections from

Barber, Elizabeth Wayland. *Women's Work: The First 20,000 Years: Women, Cloth and Society in Early Times*, Norton, 1995.

Burnham, Dorothy K. *Cut my Cote*, Royal Ontario Museum, 1973.

Hollander, Anne. *Sex and Suits*, Knopf, 1994.

Lurie, Allison. *The Language of Clothes*, First illustrated reprint ed., Henry Holt, 2000 [1981].

Phipps, Elena. *Looking at Textiles: A Guide to Technical Terms*, J. Paul Getty Museum, 2011.

Steele, Valerie. *The Corset: A Cultural History*, Yale University Press, 2001.

Materials Required: Drawing pencils, drawing paper, fabric, sewing supplies

> Types of Access Needed: Internet access suggested; library access could be used instead or in tandem.
>
> Range of Material: Egyptian to contemporary throughout the world

Shaping and Slowing Down

I teach clothing history in several contexts. In all the following cases, I am teaching clothing history as a short unit in the context of a costume or fashion design course. I have taught aspects of this unit in a fashion design course to visual arts students at LACHSA, a specialized arts high school, as one of several arts courses they can choose from. I have taught the unit as part of costume design at the college-entry level to theatre students at Los Angeles Mission College, a school in the Los Angeles Community College District. I have also taught costume design as an early college offering to both middle school students and high school students with an interest in theatre, clothing, or both.

I organize my course by focusing on garment shape and construction. I use four categories of construction – draped, square-cut, fitted, and artificially stiffened or padded garments – as a framework that students can rely on to connect any garment they encounter to a network of meaning. Each week, we discuss, draw, and construct the garment shape that is the focus of that week. My main objective is to start the students on their journey thinking about clothes as a social, economic, and cultural force. I lead students to question beauty and gender constructs, widen their perspectives on contemporary dress beyond their sphere, and apply the language of clothing coined by Alison Lurie to their dressing habits and favorite characters.

Most of the images we see around us are highly designed and crafted, and students are hungry to understand how that final image comes to be. In my course, I give the students tools to dissect any image from all sides. The construction categories and visual examples from history help them place a garment in a cultural context. Drawing teaches the students to slow down when they are studying a visual source and understand the proportions and details that go into that image. Construction helps the students see the shape of garments before they go on a body and how the body changes the shape of garments. These three analytical tools give young clothing and costume designers the basis to have control over elements of fit in both their drawings of garments and the construction of garments for physical production.

Course Objectives
- Analyze material sources including extant garments, paintings, photographs, and popular culture references for time period, geographic location, cultural identity, and occasion;
- Demonstrate awareness of different fibers and textile-making processes and their relationship to culture;
- Identify ways in which clothing has been used to express belonging, power, individuality, gender, and control, and apply these concepts to specific garments and historic silhouettes; and
- Defend the research and aesthetic choices in one's own designs.

Learning Outcomes
- Executive skills
  - Develop the communication skills necessary to work collaboratively; and
  - Understand and practice failure as part of an artistic (or a learning) process.
- Drawing skills
  - Draw an 8-head figure in proportion; and
  - Develop drawing as a tool to synthesize understanding of historical proportions with the potential to replicate them.
- Construction skills
  - Practice sewing, patterning, and garment construction.
- Analytic skills
  - Ability to analyze extant garments, images of historical garments, and pop-culture character images using the four construction categories as a jumping-off point.

Course Description

In this eight-week (24-hour) clothing history unit, a class of 15 to 25 students uses common silhouettes to learn how to think globally about modern and historical dress. We examine how four types of garment construction – draped, square-cut, fitted, and artificially stiffened or padded – iterate across some three dozen cultural moments, including India from ancient to modern, early modern Mexico, Elizabethan England, and contemporary futurism. I lead a weekly discussion, using images of that week's silhouette from across 2,500 years of clothing history and around the world. Images are paired in a

Figure 7.1 and Figure 7.2 African tunics became an important part of showing Black unity and pride in the 1960s-1970s, for the way they centered an African aesthetic. Here, an example of a Yoruba prestige robe and Jesse Jackson wearing an ikat tunic in the Pan-African colors (red, yellow, and green) in 1972

non-linear fashion to highlight connections and distinctions within the category across cultures and time.

Hands-on exercises such as drawing historical garments, designing a draped garment out of a bedsheet, and patterning a Peruvian poncho enable students to experience content through different learning modalities. These activities build their drawing and construction skills, preparing them to design (and, in my fashion class, construct) their own garments later in the course. By the end of the unit, students connect how and why different clothing silhouettes and clothing technologies developed. The module enables students to develop the tools and language they need to understand the images they find in historical research and to explain what references are at play in their later designs.

Figure 7.3 [931.12.8_1_doc20151221_ROM sleeveless upper garment Peru] This sleeveless upper garment from Peru is very similar to the Peruvian poncho the class constructs for our square-cut garment week.

Figure 7.4 Jesus Herrera takes traditional garments from all over Mexico and styles them in contemporary ways, including refashioning their gender context. Here, he is wearing a Tehuana huipil styled as if it is the most fantastic T-shirt ever, with jeans and track pants.

Source: Etsy, Jesus Herrera Styling, @thevintagejesus

This unit is suitable as part of an introductory college course and for students from 6th to 12th grade who have little or no formal exposure to fashion history or previous experience in clothing construction. The module can be tailored to fit into courses on introductory costume design, fashion design, and clothing construction. The activities also can be structured to support courses in world history.

Why I Made This Change

I started teaching costume history in 2020, in the context of a high school fashion design course at Los Angeles County High School of the Arts (LACHSA). My primary goal was for my students to have a library of inspiration to use in their contemporary fashion designs. I also wanted them to understand and be able to describe the theoretical and cultural resonances of their choices beyond the choices and inspiration of what they liked as individuals. I wanted them to have the tools to interrogate the types of clothing and images they were drawn to making. I knew that to do this, I would need to teach clothing history differently than how I learned it in the early 2000s. For one, I would be teaching this history as a short unit in a larger design class and would not have the ability to spend full classes on a particular era. Secondly, I felt a deep need to have inclusive materials that would help my students utilize inspirational material no matter where in the world or history it came from. I have always been drawn to cultures of dress outside the Western idea of "fashion" and felt the exclusion of these materials in my own coursework when I was a student. Finally, given the contemporary re-evaluation of cultural appropriation, I wanted my students to be firmly rooted in their design choices – being able both to make culturally responsible choices and to communicate the intentional resonances of their designs.

But how would I start teaching this way, which was so different from how I was taught? I thought back to a framework that my college professor had used, having learned it from her professors at Carnegie Mellon, Barbara Anderson and Cletus Anderson. They described four basic types of costume, which they called the draped, the semi-fitted, the fitted, and the artificial silhouette. They used these categories as a way to understand Western costume, but I realized that much of dress from all over the world fell into this model. I specifically linked the sari to draped clothing and the kimono to semi-fitted clothing.

Refining the Language

Over the past few years of teaching these categories, I have refined them in an effort to make them clearer and more useful to my students. For example, at first I focused on the overall effect or final silhouette of a period. Now, I focus on the construction methods of garments that together make a silhouette. I changed the framing of the concept to a construction-based model because contemporary styling – wearing a T-shirt or a pair of jeans baggy versus tight

Figure 7.5 and Figure 7.6 An example of an Egyptian "semi-fitted" tunic from 670–870 CE that is included in Western dress history courses and an example of a Chinese square-cut garment, from the Loyang Tomb (2 BCE), which evolved into hanfu in China, kimono in Japan, and hanbok in Korea.

ones, for example – had confused the idea of a fitted versus a semi-fitted silhouette. T-shirts and jeans are both fitted garments when you look at the construction of the crotch and armholes, whereas a kimono, huipil, and kaftan are not, even when they are worn very tight to the body. To make this even clearer, I now call the category under which the kimono, huipil, kaftan, and many historical Western shirts fall the "square-cut" garment. This language emphasizes that it is the reliance on loom widths as well as the mostly straight pattern lines that make this category what it is. I also changed the category that Anderson and Anderson call the "artificial silhouette" to "artificially stiffened or padded garments." This language emphasizes the ways in which the silhouette is created. When the categories are more specific, the student is able to access and apply them more easily to a garment they are examining or designing.

Adaptability

One unique quality of my approach is its adaptability. I adapt this course to the population I am teaching. For the early college offerings at both the middle school and high school levels, the goal is to foster interest in design, visual culture, and performance among young people. The course is an opportunity for these students to discover what is possible in the fields of dress history, costume design, and character design and to find out if they have an interest in this arena. My goals are similar with my college students, but we are able to dive deeper. The college students often have a stronger grasp on readings and are more self-directed, which allows me to add a critique session discussing the students' drawings to each class.

In the fashion design class, the emphasis is on giving students tools to analyze their inspirations and learning construction. In this course, I focus the first half of class on image-based discussion over four weeks, one for each construction method. I also favor one large, full-scale square-cut garment project that replaces the weekly drawings and smaller sewing projects. I use this project to teach students sewing basics on an easy garment shape and allow them to adapt the proportions to their bodies and design. More advanced students have the opportunity to practice zero-waste clothing design on complex square-cut patterns.

As I have taught this course, I have found it best to make ample time for students to practice the construction techniques in class supervised. Students, even those who have not taken drawing before, have been able to draw the week's silhouette from the images given.

Drawing and Critique

With my college students, I have found that giving the drawings as homework outside class and beginning each class session with an active critique provides the students with an opportunity to apply the concepts from the garment shape discussions from previous weeks. The critiques strengthen their communication abilities and bolster their confidence in their drawings. I have also noticed the students making connections between categories through these critique sessions.

Figures 7.7 and 7.8 Two student drawings of Fujiwara Court dress. When students compare their drawings of the same image, it helps them see the unique point of view each person has and will apply to their costume designs later in the course.

Sources: Figure 7.7: Natalie Arrendondo; Figure 7.8: Jacob Padilla

The drawings in this section of the course are from historical research, by which I mean historical paintings or photos that show the full body of a person or mannequin wearing an example of that week's silhouette. The students are asked to copy the body of the person wearing the garment, as well as the garment itself, as faithfully as possible, paying particular attention to the proportions that define the garment. I give students three image choices in a particular construction category – one male, one historical female, and one contemporary. This provides them with a chance to focus on a garment example best suited to their interest. For example, during the square-cut garment week, the options are Japanese Fujiwara court dress, Frida Kahlo wearing a huipil, and Afghani-Dutch fashion blogger Ruba Zai in a Dolce and Gabbana abaya and hijab. I tell students to spend 30 minutes drawing. They can either spend this time on one drawing or do multiple tries and submit them all to show their progress.

Critique in Practice

Drawing from *Liz Lerman's Critical Response Process,* a guide to teaching critique, I ask students: What do you notice? What associations do you make with what you are seeing compared to other things in the world? Is there anything surprising? I ask students to refrain from giving opinions in the critique session because we are focusing on making connections between the work and ideas from our discussions and readings and material culture from outside the class. It is in this section that students gain the most confidence. The students learn that even when they don't like their drawings, they are still communicating ideas to other people. They learn that they already have the ability to make connections that matter to their classmates. Making connections to the reading and to outside media like television and film shows them how the garments in each discussion continue to ramify in their lives.

Assessment
Primary forms of assessment: Drawing and construction projects. One midterm presentation.

Syllabus Details
This course is broken up into two major units: Unit 1: The Language of Clothes and an Introduction to Clothing Motifs and Unit 2: Designing Costumes for a Play.

Unit 1: The Language of Clothes and an Introduction to Clothing Motifs

In this unit, you will develop an understanding of how clothes speak – the many symbols that each item of clothing communicates. You will see different examples of the four main ways clothing is constructed throughout history and across the world. Using the images I present to you as a jumping-off point, you will create life-size and miniature garments that apply the historical knowledge you have gained. Finally, you will examine a favorite character and present to the class an in-depth analysis of that character's full look including hair, makeup, and clothing.

Midterm
- One presentation assignment: In which you examine a favorite character and present to the class an in-depth analysis of that character's full look including hair, makeup, and clothing: 100 points;
- Four construction assignments: In which you create life-size or miniature garments in the construction style of the week: 100 points total (25 points each); and
- Four drawing assignments: In which you copy historical research to gain a better understanding of the clothes: 100 points total (25 points each).

Weekly Outlook
- Each week, we will tackle a topic and explore that topic through discussion, group work, and hands-on activities such as drawing and working with fabric;
- You will have weekly assignments in the form of readings, research, drawings and renderings, constructing garments, and completing costume paperwork;
- Any in-class assignments (assignments you will have time to start in class) and homework assignments will be due at the beginning of class the following week;
- You must bring the work of the previous week(s) to each class as you will continue to build on that work in each class;
- You will be regularly sharing and discussing your work and that of your classmates;
- You will have two presentations: One midterm presentation and one large design project culminating in a presentation; and
- Everything that is due will have a date and will be listed on the Canvas calendar and your To-Do list.

Unit Plan and Projects, First Eight Weeks

Table 7.1 Syllabus Calendar

Week	Topic and Goals	In-Class Assignment	Homework Assigned
1	What Is Costume Design? Goals: Introduce ourselves to each other, the course themes, and goals. Set individual goals for the semester. Identify, classify, and discuss historical costume, contemporary costume, runway fashion, street fashion, ceremonial clothing, and cosplay. We will work together to define what it means to design costumes for performance and how it differs from designing clothing in a fashion context.	Find visual examples of historical, contemporary, stage, and runway clothes. Classify the images you find into costume, fashion, everyday, and ceremonial. What are the similarities and differences? Are they hard categories, or do they bleed into each other? Video: "How a Costume Designer Creates an Iconic Look"	Reading: Lurie, Alison. *The Language of Clothes*, Henry Holt, 2000. Chapter 1: "Clothing as a Sign System" (3–36) Reading; Barber, Elizabeth Wayland. *Women's Work: The First 20,000 Years: Women, Cloth and Society in Early Times*, Norton, 1995. Introduction (17–25), Chapter 1: A Tradition with a Reason (29–41) Assignment: Choose a favorite character and put it on Padlet. Respond to another classmate's favorite character with one or two associations that you make to the clothes of that character.

(*Continued*)

Table 7.1 Continued

Week	Topic and Goals	In-Class Assignment	Homework Assigned
2	Crafting Presence: Clothes, Textiles and Sewing Questions: What does it mean for clothes to "speak"? How can using the idea of clothing as a sign system help us read what clothes say and communicate with clothes? Goals: Examine the reasons people wear clothes and our individual and societal relationships to those reasons. Understand how cloth is made, including the tools associated with it, and why we think of the practice of making clothing as gendered. Learn to tie a knot, thread a needle, and sew a straight line.	Hand sew a straight line using the backstitch.	Reading: Hollander, Anne. *Sex and Suits*, Knopf, 1994. Introduction: "Sex and Modern Form" (3–13) Assignment: Draw a full-body (head to toe) self-portrait or a portrait of a friend or family member. You can draw this using a mirror or a photo. You don't need to be standing. Be prepared to discuss in class.
3	Fitted Garments BRING A T-SHIRT TO CUT UP. Goals: Understand the development of technologies that make fitted clothing possible, including tailoring and stretch fabrics. Examine the suit, the T-shirt, and athletic fashions. Interrogate the connection between fitted garments and ideas of democracy, equality, and modernity.	Lay out pattern for, cut out, and construct a hoodie for a doll.	Reading: Burnham, Dorothy K. *Cut My Cote*, Royal Ontario Museum, 1973. Introduction and "Garments From Loom Lengths Without Sewing" (2–6) Reading: Phipps, Elena. *Looking at Textiles: A Guide to Technical Terms*, J. Paul Getty Museum, 2011. Introduction (1–12). Assignment: Finish sewing all your hoodie body parts together, close the sleeves, and sew your hood parts together. We will learn to connect them next week.

An Abridged Clothing History in Four Construction Techniques ◆ 115

| 4 | Draped Garments
BRING A FLAT SHEET TO CLASS and ALL DOLL HOODIE MATERIALS.
Questions: Why does it matter who made a specific image? How can we use this to understand the development of the Western sarong and its relation to wrapped rectangles worn around the world?
Goals: Identify ancient and contemporary draped (sometimes called wrapped) styles of dress and the ways in which they are interconnected. Consider how draped garments have influenced other types of dress we've seen. Examine the importance of knowing the artist/image maker when looking at research. | Choose one of the draped garments presented in class to recreate OR design your own using yourself or a classmate as a model.
Finish doll hoodie: Connect hood and sleeves to body. | Reading: Burnham, Dorothy K. *Cut My Cote*, Royal Ontario Museum, 1973. "The Beginning of Sewn Garments" (7–8).
Assignment: Draw one of the given examples of a person wearing a draped garment. Be prepared to discuss in class.
Assignment: Your completed doll hoodie |
| 5 | Square-Cut and T-Shaped Garments
BRING A LARGE PIECE OF FABRIC TO CLASS.
Goals: Classify what makes a square-cut garment different from a draped or fitted garment. Examine the development of square-cut garments such as the Japanese kimono, the Mexican huipil, the Middle Eastern kaftan, and the West African boubou. | Practice laying out a pattern from a diagram with written directions. Make a poncho for a doll. | Reading: Steele, Valerie. *The Corset: A Cultural History*, Yale University Press, 2001. Chapter 1: "Steel and Whalebone: Fashioning the Aristocratic Body" (1–33).
Assignment: Draw one of the given examples of a person wearing a square-cut garment. Be prepared to discuss in class.
Assignment: Your completed poncho |

(*Continued*)

Table 7.1 Continued

Week	Topic and Goals	In-Class Assignment	Homework Assigned
6	Artificially Stiffened or Padded Garments BRING UNCONVENTIONAL MATERIALS. (Some examples are hangers, dry food, bowls, umbrellas, baskets, paper plates or cups, paper towel tubes, toilet paper.) Goals: Examine the role of underwear in the development of artificially stiffened or padded garments. Identify the reasons that people have chosen to wear these garments and the continued interest in them in contemporary fashion. Analyze the relationship these garments have to understanding how our concepts of gender have shifted over time.	Make a wearable sculpture that captures the sense of the artificially stiffened or padded garments of history using unconventional materials. This can be doll size or life size.	Assignment: Draw one of the given examples of a person wearing artificially stiffened or padded garments. Be prepared to discuss in class. Assignment: Your completed wearable sculpture
7	Questions: How do you figure out where an image came from or what inspired it? What are the resources you can use to make your best guess? Goals: To examine our favorite characters for clues of culture and time period using garment shape and online databases as a resource.	Use FIT's fashion history timeline to determine historical and cultural influences on your favorite character. Continue work on favorite character presentations as time permits.	Favorite character presentations due next week

8	Presentations – Favorite Character
Goals: To hear and discuss favorite character presentations. To recognize the knowledge we have gained thus far in the semester and how it has contributed to our insights into characters that other costume and character designers have created. To practice presenting our ideas and contributing thoughtful responses.

Source: Lena Sands, 2022

Class Flow

Table 7.2 At the collegiate level, I set up a three-hour class to include a critique, a lecture/discussion, and a hands-on activity time. For example, the week in which we focus on square-cut garments looks like this.

Sample Week: College	
8:50–9:00	Check in, everyone puts out their drawings of draped garments
9:00–10:00	Drawing critique of draped garment drawings from photo/painting observation
10:00–10:10	Break
10:10–11:00	Discussion with slide show of the square-cut garment; this includes showing pattern pieces for square-cut garments
11:00–12:00	Make a Peruvian poncho for a doll. Emphasis is on how to read and enlarge a historical pattern, how to use a ruler and center a line, and what seam allowance is. By the end of class, we should have our fabric cut and our ponchos marked. We will sew them next class.

Table 7.3 At the high school level, I teach this as a 1.5 hour class twice a week. The first class of the week is a discussion section, and the second class of the week is a lab.

Sample Week: High School	
Tuesday	Discussion Day
9:40–10:00	Share questions about the reading
10:00–10:55	Square-cut garment lecture/discussion
10:55–11:00	Wrap up, homework
Thursday	Lab Day
8:30–8:40	Hand out materials
8:40–9:10	Demonstration of Peruvian poncho: Explain selvedge, how to use a ruler and square a line, seam allowance
9:10–10:00	Students mark out ponchos and prepare to sew
10:00–10:10	Clean up

Student Responses

The tactile, hands-on aspect of the class is particularly useful with younger students, who learn best through doing and are motivated by projects.

- Sense of achievement with each drawing and garment made;
- Community-building aspect of critiquing each other's work and making connections;
- Building self-esteem that they can see and understand period research and feel that their viewpoints matter;
- Connections made to home cultures and an excitement to share about those cultures in the context of the class;
- Aha moments
  - That women's legs were barely seen before the 1910s – "But that's so recent";
  - Considerations of the suit as a democratic garment and who is granted power from it (including discussions of Obama's khaki suit and Hillary Clinton' pant suits);
- Excitement at learning to sew; and
- 100% of my student reviewers would recommend the class to others.

8

Examining and Creating Connections in Costume History Through Cultural Intersections and Alternative Assessment Models

Sarah Mosher

Course Description

This course focuses on the ways that costume transfers and transforms at cultural intersections, whether it be through conquest and appropriation, mutual trade, or places where built and natural environments connect or conflict. The Western dress timeline serves as a loose framework to support this exploration, pulling in societies that paralleled certain ideas or aesthetics or were chronologically concurrent. This allows us to discuss cultural connections but also cultural parallels that existed outside of known interaction. We interrogate the relationship of humans to their physical environment and how they locate themselves within that context through dress and decoration by looking at the sourcing of fibers, dyestuffs, and technologies that support the built world of clothing and accessories. We ask difficult questions about environmental justice and cultural competence that contribute to productive discourse and require us to confront our own biases with regard to attire, appearance, and the production of goods for adornment.

> School: Baylor University
> Department: Theatre Arts
> Student Level/Description: Upper division, major specific
> Class Size: 10-15 Students
> Hours/Week: 3
> Format: In person
> Text or Core Materials: All texts were supplied by the instructor or accessed online or through the library. In the case of hands-on work, students located what they needed using the resources familiar to them.
> Types of Access Needed: Online library access, Canvas LMS

Like so many of us, I took a history of costume course based on a standardized textbook and measured by basic identification tests in my undergraduate years, with lectures and assignments from that same text in different courses. I took a history of costume course based on the same text and methodology in graduate school, engaged with content from it in another class, created a presentation based on the first chapter, and then used it as a source when teaching quick overviews to undergraduate students. In my first academic job as an adjunct, I used it as a source when teaching overviews and then was contracted to teach a history of costume course based on this specific text and model for a mix of fashion and theatre students. As I repeatedly interacted with this version of costume history, I grew restless. There were so many stories missing from the text, most of which belonged to people from the global majority, whose cultures were the places of origin for many items and ideas appropriated by the Western world as fashion items. I began incorporating these stories where I could, assigning presentations on the Persian empire and their style of decoration for textiles, the silk industry origins and history in China, the cotton industry of India, the use of indigo in various places around the world, the weaving techniques of groups in the Andes highlands, etc. Even so, the class still felt too tied to this specific delineation of Western dress, with everything else stuck on the periphery.

The approach to content then had to be shifted and made both broader and more deliberate to ensure that students were exposed to a more global understanding of dress within the limits of our one semester together.

Questions of social and environmental justice were important to me and were also being critically examined and explored culturally, so they would serve as a throughline for the content and our conversations in class. Clearly just adding content was not going to work, so in addition to sourcing other texts, journal articles, popular articles, videos, and tangible artifacts, I also began the process of interrogating the form of the class.

Since I began teaching, I started asking questions about the educational system, built-in assumptions about student-teacher hierarchies, and if there were better approaches to engage students as individuals, recognizing their distinct skill and knowledge levels as they approach the class. I did not have this level of vocabulary or understanding of the issues – just the itch to reach my students more equitably and get each of them to engage their own creativity and find intrinsic motivation for the work. I was concerned about the rising impulse in students not to turn things in because they were afraid they weren't perfect or to procrastinate for the same reason. Sometimes students were overwhelmed and felt unprepared and thus decided not to show up. Students needed structured scaffolding of low-stakes assignments to lead them to self-directed creative projects; paradoxically, they needed both more structure and more freedom. I have tried a variety of methods over the years, like offering low-stakes assignments with simple but objective rubrics and offering students the option to redo assignments as many times as desired to get their preferred grade, as long as the original assignment was turned in on time. I saw the application of these methods as a win-win situation, with students having the opportunity to practice their skills, as well as having more agency in the determination of their final grades, which was appealing to them.

I began to explore the work of Augusto Boal and the Theatre of the Oppressed,[1] which also opened my awareness to Paulo Freire and *The Pedagogy of the Oppressed*.[2] Freire's thoughts and the way he offered a critical lens to educational systems really resonated with me and gave me courage to shift the paradigm in my classes in radical ways. Even more crucially, the work of bell hooks[3] and her critical examination of Freire's work helped me dig in deeper. At the same time, a friend of mine and fellow professor at Baylor introduced me to standards-based grading (SBG). There was something about this that connected with the way my brain works and the goals our department has for our theatre students over their whole time at the university. I tried structuring assessment models that explored SBG in my skills classes to mixed success. Some students embraced the model while others were very resistant to this shift in expectations. I still believe the core of this idea is of value and am finding ways to refine it and make it my own, mixing it with assessment methods students find more familiar, in effect scaffolding the assessment model so students will go on the journey and see the benefit at a pace they are comfortable with. In the fall of 2021, the Academy for Teaching and Learning at Baylor offered a workshop on ungrading. I reached out to the facilitator, and we met for coffee to talk about the various modalities and how to flex those models for different class types. In reading *Ungrading*, a compilation of essays edited by Susan D. Blum,[4] I was fascinated with the variety of approaches and found a few that felt like they would apply well to my upcoming history of costume course.

In thinking about who this class was geared towards, which was upper-class theatre design majors who chose this elective, I knew I could ask them to participate in their own education more by challenging them and empowering them with new assessment models.

I also wanted to rethink the course content, but I had only so much time to make this happen. I decided to allow myself some stepping stones, continuing to tie the course content loosely to the Western dress timeline because I knew I could make the connections between cultures happen more smoothly knowing the timeline well. This allowed me to explore the content at the same time as my students, letting us go on a journey together, while still meeting some student expectations about learning Western costume terminology and its application to their work in theatre. It felt important in the context of the curricular culture of our department, the focus of which is professional preparation with a strong aesthetic emphasis in realism, to maintain some connection to Western costume systems so students would be prepared to design shows in our season. We could pursue this aspect of costume history while also exploring new content together as a class and learning the skills that would allow students to research multi-modality with any content they might encounter.

Course Objectives
- Identify the history of Western costumes from ancient to contemporary times;
- Express an understanding of cultural and historic influences affecting clothing of the past and present;
- Identify the importance of historic fashion in today's fashion;
- Demonstrate an academic writing style related to textile and clothing research areas; and
- Research costume-related questions independently and apply that understanding outside the classroom context.

Learning Outcomes

Students are given the opportunity to create their own measurable goals for the semester, which they tailor to their interests and to the potential application of skills and knowledge gained. The model of assessment depends on the students engaging, evaluating, and reflecting on a regular basis, particularly around their approach to the materials. For example, some students want to quickly name off items based on visual identification, whereas others want to build up a toolkit for themselves that helps them research and navigate costume construction techniques and approaches, which can be as precise or theatrical as needed in the context. This self-assessment format, fueled by conversational feedback from me on Canvas, keeps the learning objectives and outcomes at the forefront of students' minds throughout the course. Students can use these goals to inform how they take notes, how they study the material, and what research project they select to investigate during this course.

Table 8.1 Syllabus Calendar

Week	Class Topic	Readings Due	Assignment Due
1	Course overview		
	Quiz on Chapter 1	Chapter 1	Goal setting
2	Quiz review; return goal-setting documents with notes	Ancient MENA, China	
	China and Persians	Persians	
3	Greeks, Minoans	Minoans, Greeks, Romans	
	Romans, Byzantium	Byzantium	
4	Online quiz	The Berbers, East Africa	Paper proposal draft
	Library visit		Paper proposal
5	The Americas, the Berbers, and East Africa	Mesoamerica, Ancient Andes	
	Digging deeper	Aztec sumptuary laws	Week 5 – Goal reflection

Week	Class Topic	Readings Due	Assignment Due
6	Late Middle Ages	Late Middle Ages	
	India	India, chintz	
7	Renaissance and Tudor	Italian Renaissance	
	Online quiz	Northern Renaissance	Paper outline
8	Spring Break		
	Spring Break		
9	17th century	17th century, West Africa	
	Colonization and dress	Indigo	Paper poster sessions
10	18th century	18th century	
	1790–1850	"The Ancient Fabric" (BBC)	Week 10 goal reflection
11	1850–1870		
	Bustle and Edwardian		Paper draft 1
12	Diadeloso		
	1920s and 1930s		
13	1940s		
	1950s		Paper draft 2
14	1960s Activity Day		
	1970s Activity Day		
15	1980s Activity Day		
	1990s Activity Day		Week 15 goal reflection
16	2000s Activity Day		Final paper
	Topic wild card		Final goal reflection

Source: Sarah Mosher, 2022

Shifting Assessment

In laying out the course, I knew that the biggest shift for my students would be the assessment model. It was crucial to me that I present it with transparency and vulnerability by clearly laying out the benefits to them both for the semester and for life beyond the university. As a result, I devoted my first class period to sharing the assessment model and giving the students a good snapshot of what to expect in the course so they could opt in or out – they all opted in. I explained that, as this was an upper division course, the students were close to graduation and would need to investigate their own intrinsic motivations in order to successfully navigate the professional world, and this assessment model would allow them exercise this skill. Their interrogating their personal goals for this course and then developing some specific measures for themselves allowed them and me to direct their focus over the semester through conversational assessment. I outline this process in more detail later in this chapter.

To help scaffold their comfort with this conversational style of assessment, they read Chapter 1 of Tortora,[5] and in the next class period, they took an essay quiz on the content, which I then responded to conversationally to help them with context, show curiosity, and probe into their answers. My responses were typically modeling curiosity about their replies and my own authentic thoughts and observations on the content and lifting up comments made by the students that were especially astute or that drew connections in interesting ways. I tried to avoid offering critique that would indicate I had an answer in mind that was "right," although I did offer questions that might challenge them to dig deeper. Upon reading my responses, they then reflected on their performance on the quiz, including their thinking as they answered the question, their method of taking notes and engaging with the reading material, and their ability to draw connections. The final part of their reflection was to assign themselves a letter grade based on their reflection, my notes, and their personal course goals. This grade was then recorded for the assignment in our LMS, except in rare cases in which I wanted to challenge their assessment and give them an opportunity to respond. In these cases, I had to adjust the grade up as the students were harder on themselves than I might have been.

This method of essay quizzes was used through the semester to test learning and to help students reflect on their progress and approach by looking at them in the context of specific questions. As we progressed, the questions became broader and allowed for more autonomy. For example, a question from the first quiz was: "What challenges does Tortora point out as being a part of researching costume history? What are her recommendations for being a cautious and thoughtful researcher?" A question from the Week 4 quiz: "Environment has played a huge role historically in the way people dress. As you think about the cultures we have explored so far, how has geographical environment played a role specifically? Select two cultures to compare and contrast here." Students had more agency to select the examples they wanted to investigate and to dig into their own personal research interests, reflecting on the content they had highlighted in their reading and investigating.

Where content was concerned, the calendar loosely followed the Western dress timeline, but I used a variety of readings to offer context and explore cultural contact and connections. For instance, in the second week, we read the Tortora section on the ancient Middle East and North Africa (MENA),[6] the Anawalt chapter on China,[7] and Harvey's chapter on Persian clothing,[8] as well as exploring popular articles on Chinese hanfu revival,[9] makeup and cosmetics in ancient Egypt,[10] and critical contributions of the Persians[11] and a contemporary news article on Arnold Putra wearing far-right paramilitary attire at Paris Fashion Week.[12] The breadth of this content allowed students to wrestle with questions about what is connected and what is not between disparate cultures and times. It also challenged them to take the concept of costume history and recognize that contemporary life is both shaping and being shaped by it.

The connections between the cultures we investigated fell into two broad categories. One was the direct influence of the dress of one culture on another culture, and the other was parallel styles, techniques, or decorative motifs shared between cultures that don't seem to have had contact. In exploring the direct influences, we looked at various forms of contact like trade and conquest, examining the ways in which influence moves. We considered the context of each culture in that time and place to discover how that influenced what they wore and how, in some cases, that primed them for adopting or appropriating. The trade and subsequent commodification and extermination through overbearing demand for fine muslin from India were examples we explored while simultaneously looking at the Western European proclivity for the novel and the colonial mindset that led to the exhaustion of supply and subjugation of the people responsible for cultivation and production. When we studied cultures without proof of contact, we looked at the similarities we witnessed and explored the ways in which environment, time, and place might have influenced those decisions, such as the way that indigo has been used by the Miao people in China to burnish their textiles bearing a striking resemblance to a method used in Western Africa by the Hausa.

Students engaged in their own research project on the topic of their choice over the course of the semester, culminating in a paper on the subject. (They also had the opportunity to create an artifact and write a shorter paper.) This allowed them to put their research skills to the test and work autonomously with support. There were multiple checkpoints built in to ensure success, including first meeting with our librarian about their topic proposal to ensure they could find what they needed, then having the librarian sign off on the proposal before they turned it in. Students also created posters that were publicly displayed in the theatre lobby, which provided a great checkpoint to help them feel more confident about their work and also forced them to articulate the key points of their topic in a succinct way, both verbally and visually. All the stops of this project are listed later in this chapter.

Environmental justice and the relationship between dress and the sustainability of materials and labor were woven throughout the course. In every discussion, we explored ways in which the natural environment of the culture affected dress, and students began to develop a nuanced way of evaluating the role of environment, moving from the obvious concerns of dressing to protect from the climate to aspects of place identity and land-based cultural heritage expressed in appearance. The students embraced these questions, and the breadth of connections was interesting. Some pointed out the example of ultra-fine cotton muslin production as a place-based cultural heritage in dress while others cited weaving colors and patterns in Andean textiles, which showed great specificity of place through the unique patterns of each craftsperson. Through these discussions, students developed a curiosity for their own environment and considered their relationships with the land in central Texas. They asked about natural dyeing and expressed curiosity about dye sources native to central Texas. With the flexibility of the course, we were able to decide collaboratively to spend time on this topic, researching options, gathering plants for dyestuffs, and ultimately spending a class period dyeing wool using what we had gathered. (See Figure 8.1) This experience gave the students an appreciation for the process of color textiles and also reconnected them with the land around them, opening up new lines of inquiry for them to consider questions of environmental justice.

We expanded on this interest in the land around them and the materiality of textiles, by scheduling our final exam period as a field trip to a local farm where students learned to spin wool into yarn. This experience was paid for by our department and students showed great enthusiasm and interest in the process, with a few purchasing more wool to take home and turn to yarn, continuing the exploration beyond the class.

As we started the semester, students shared what they hoped to get out of the class and what motivated them to take it. In our department, the class is one of two required options for our BFA design and technology students, but I also had a performance major and a film major in my class; clearly, there were more than graduation requirements motivating the students. I shifted

Figure 8.1 Students and faculty dyeing with bluebonnets donated by a local farm
Source: Sarah Mosher, 2021

the focus from "learn and memorize" to "learn to research," shared my thinking, and then let students write up their own personal goals and objectives for the course, which allowed them to tailor their interactions with the material to their desired outcomes. I talked about what my expectations were, how the class would function, and how assessment worked; I then set the provocation to the students to write up three specific goals for the course for themselves. Each goal had to be specific to them, and they had to identify how we would measure that goal, but it could be something as simple as "I want to get at least a B in this course" as long as they outlined how they would achieve that (an idea that came from Clarissa Sorensen-Unruh's essay in the ungrading book).[13]

They submitted their goals to me through our LMS (Canvas), and I responded with thoughts and observations on their goals, prompting more specificity in some places, helping them draw connections between what they wrote and how we would structure our class in others. We revisited these goals about every four or five weeks. Students would read over their goals and criteria for success and evaluate their progress at each milestone. They considered whether they were hitting their own expectations for each goal, if there were ways they could adjust their work behaviors to better focus on their goal, and in quite a few cases if their goal or measures of success still fit. A student who is a costume technician set a goal to learn all the structural construction types over history and realized after the first few weeks that learning how to research construction for a given time would be more valuable as a skill set since it could apply to anything they might encounter. I encouraged and reinforced this realization, and for the remainder of the semester, that student found some great ways to implement this new goal.

During their goal assessment, students assessed themselves overall, suggesting their current letter grade in the course based on their performance on their goals. I then offered feedback and perspective in response and either agreed with their assessment or offered a different perspective. I typically agreed with their assessments; when I didn't, it was generally because the student was being too harsh on themselves, and I would have to offer a higher grade.

Initial Goal Setting

Identify three main goals for yourself for this semester. They should be related to the content of this class and be as specific and realistic as possible.

Your focus may be on learning terms for costume history, for example. In that case, a goal might be "Be able to identify by name the key garments and accessories the help define each period and culture presented. Secondarily, be able to explain what they are and why they are key to the period/culture."

It could also be related to your personal performance in this class. For example: "I will dedicate time to learning to identify items and challenge myself by looking for other examples as practice."

It should also be realistic, so a goal may look like this: "I will pass this class so I can graduate. Achieving a C in this class will meet my goal. I will discover what work I need to stay on top of to achieve a C and prioritize appropriately."

To turn in your goals, either copy and paste into the text field or upload a pdf of your goals.

> **Goal Assessment, Week 5**
>
> Look at your original goals. How are you doing in relation to your goals? Where are you seeing success? What has been a challenge? Where do you need support? Now that you have been in class for a few weeks, is there anything you would like to amend in your goals statement?
>
> 1. Reflect on the questions above and write up your responses.
> 2. Confirm your goals by adding them in again or updating them as desired.
> 3. Based on your current work, what grade would you be earning at this time and why?
> 4. What adjustments would you like to make to your workflow?
> 5. Is there anything I could do to better support you?
>
> Copy and paste your responses into the text field or upload a pdf of your responses.

Assessment Model

Conversational Assessment

At this advanced level, I am interested in your ability to set your own learning goals, assess your own work, reflect on your learning, and plan for your next steps. Because of this, we will work together as a team to assess work in this class.

You will set three specific goals for yourself for this course and continue to manage your workload, note taking, and evaluation with these in mind.

Quizzes will help you test your knowledge and progress, and we will work together to determine your grade on each one. These grades will be entered into Canvas but will NOT be factored into your final grade.

You will create a term paper with multiple check points to give you a chance to go deep on your understanding in one area. Each step will give you a chance to scaffold your knowledge and skills in costume research.

By the last part of the semester, your skills will be stronger, and you will become the subject matter expert, leading activity days for your topic and time period to engage me and your classmates in the material. You can be as creative or straightforward as you like.

Your reflection on your goals will be the critical aspect of determining your final grade. As we progress, you will give me reflections on your progress with well-supported cases for your current grade. At the end of the semester, we will look over all your work together as well as your final reflection, and you will make a case for your final grade. If I disagree, we will have a conversation, and I will make my case, then you can counter before the final grade is submitted.

> Flexibility and humility are key disciplines to exercise if you are planning this type of assessment model. I had to check my systemically ingrained assumptions constantly and focus on the growth and knowledge the students brought to class each day.

Sample Project

Research Project Assignment

Proposal – You will turn in a one-page proposal including the following:

1. The topic you chose and why you are interested in the topic. This should be your paper title and paper subtitle with as much detail as necessary;
2. Significant themes and an outline of your paper structure;
3. Preliminary works cited list with MLA-style citation (five sources); and
4. The signature of our librarian, Sha Towers, showing that you discussed the topic with him and are on the right track with your resources.

Outline – You will turn in a multi-page outline with fleshed-out points. This should show the structure of your paper and how you plan to develop each area. This is used to mark your progress and development. Include the following:

1. An outline showing your main points and your sub-points with notations on where you will be using your references; and
2. An updated reference list with additional citations.

Poster Session – To exercise your knowledge and check how clearly you can communicate your topic to others, you will present your topic during our class poster session.

1. Prepare a visual presentation. This should be presented on a single self-supporting poster board or foam core. The science fair boards are great for this. Be sure to consider your layout and make sure it matches the content. Text should be legible even at a foot or so away. Include your name, the title of your paper, and good visual references;
2. Be ready to speak about your topic for two to three minutes. This means just hitting the highlights. These can be the more critical points or fun facts that people will find compelling. This will exercise your ability to filter for critical information;
3. You will be responding with one question for each of your peers, so be ready to pay attention and take notes; and
4. Before the presentation, upload a pdf with your talking point notes and a photo of your board.

Paper Draft 1 – Drafts help keep you on track and allow for feedback throughout the process.

1. Draft 1 should be at least five to six pages in length. This could be a little bit in each area, ready to flesh out, or a fleshed-out beginning and notes for the remainder of the paper. Proceed in the way that works for you;
2. Include an updated works cited list with additional references you are using;
3. Include a note at the end stating what you focused on for this draft and what your plans are for next steps (be specific); and
4. Upload your draft as a pdf. Your next draft will be submitted with Turnitin, so you can catch any issues before the final.

Paper Draft 2 – Drafts help keep you on track and allow for feedback throughout the process.

1. Draft 2 should be full length. Every area should be fleshed out at this point;
2. Include an updated works cited list with additional references you are using;
3. Include a note at the end stating what you focused on for this draft and what your plans are for next steps (be specific); and
4. Your draft will be submitted with Turnitin, so you can catch any issues before the final.

Final Paper Guidelines – Include the following in your paper:

1. Introduction to state your topic, thesis, historical relevance, potential impact on modern dress, and what the reader should take away from your paper;
2. Body to flesh out your outline. For ease of planning, you should try to focus on three main themes that you can support with your research. Include citations of your sources and create smooth transitions from one thought to another. You should include at least five images in your paper, properly cited from reputable sources to support your writing;
3. Conclusion in which you will tie together all of your themes and explain how they support your original thesis and implications for further research or direct application;
4. Works cited to cite in full all sources. Include a minimum of five books, two academic journals, five images, and at least eight additional sources, all of which are cited in the body of your paper. Consistent citation and formatting must be followed; and
5. Submit your paper to Turnitin online through Canvas.

Curricular Correlations

This version of ungrading seemed much more effective than other attempts in my previous courses, so I have applied this conversational assessment model to my other upper-division courses, adding in a bit of scaffolding to support their engagement, such as offering rubrics to measure their technical application of skills in an objective manner. I foresee continuing to test and apply these methods across all my classes to one degree or another. I have also been sharing these methods and learnings with on-campus colleagues who are interested in trying new methods of engaged learning.

As the focus moved organically towards questions of sustainability and place-based material sourcing in this rendition of the course, my chair and I realized it would be an ideal addition to the environmental humanities minor newly approved at Baylor. Opening up this course to the College of Arts and Sciences in this way provides some interesting challenges and opportunities the next time it is offered, and being included in the minor will mean that the course will be offered more frequently. The benefit of the conversational grading method is that personalization is built in so that students from other disciplines can be on the same footing as students from the department whom I've worked with before. The challenge I will potentially face here is the need to scale up from my current class size. Class sizes under 10 have made this personalized assessment manageable, but I will need to consider more efficient methods if I need to scale up considerably, and those methods still need to adhere to the spirit of the work.

Partnering with my colleague in art history to host a creative arts experience (CAE) on Minoan weaving provided a wonderful experience in working across disciplines and allowed us to feature a loom built and used by my students in the class. Students owning responsibility for various components and then showcasing their knowledge and experience to peers were very empowering to them, and the audience response was so enthusiastic that I am encouraged to attempt this again with better planning and structure, which will benefit us all! It is hoped that we can continue to develop our connection with art and art history since we share a building with them, and the intersections between our work are many. The next step may be to work with students from one of their classes so students are working interdepartmentally. Other colleagues have been encouraged by this example of coursework leading to a CAE and are brainstorming their own versions in our department as well as in art and art history.

Based on the visibility of the projects that came out of this class, including the CAE and public presentation of the research posters, I have been approached by a couple of graduate students who are interested in taking the course. Encouraged by positive feedback from the former students and by the framing of personal goal setting, the graduate students are eager to engage in the content at their own level. I am optimistic that this will allow a deeper level of engagement using this self-directed methodology and am already considering a real-life application project that would connect our graduate students to the local community and require an exercise in cultural humility and recognition of other forms of knowledge keeping. The potential impact of this is exciting, and it is only possible because of the flexible format of the assessment model.

Overall, I was pleasantly surprised by how well this risk paid off, and it gave me courage to implement these methods in my other classes as well. In particular, the assessment model and student involvement were very successful, as were the independent research project and the CAE group project, which served our university and demonstrated to my students how much they knew about a topic.

Students who have taken this course have now gone into working on productions in the department and have demonstrated more independence in the research aspect, leading to more accuracy but also to more diversity of research. It was an unexpected benefit to see how much more creative the students have become in their approach and how much more detail oriented.

Figure 8.2 Students warping the reproduction Minoan standing loom that they build in preparation for their demonstration to 50 students from across the university

Now, this is only one class, so I am curious to see if this pattern holds up with the next group of students, but it has been heartening to hear how often this course has come up in discussion among the students and how meaningful it has been to them. Two of my students were speaking the other day and said that this was their favorite course they have taken, with one noting that they had the opportunity to use and share their crafting skills from other contexts in a practice as research context, which was very empowering!

In planning the next iteration of this course and based on what I've learned so far, I have a few goals in mind: I would like to move away from the Western timeline a little more, create a structured service learning project that we can work on over time, and adjust my assessment techniques for the final research project.

I plan to move away from the Western timeline a little more by leaning into the exploration of cultural intersections, spending more time on each study of such contact or parallel so we can dig in deeper with our research skills. Instead of a broad overview, starting with a case study that we walk through together, reading content, watching videos, doing hands-on practice as research in the classroom, and listening to first-person accounts, we can learn a great deal about a topic and also use that experience to talk about research frameworks for the class. I am hopeful that this may encourage some practice as research choices in their final research project as well, embracing various forms of knowing and understanding. I am considering preparing a variety of case studies of various intersections and letting students help decide where we go after we have a few completed. I will continue to revisit a database I have created of a wide variety of sources pertaining to questions of costume history to look for fun connections I can explore with the students and to see when new articles pop up that can supplement my current content.

Crafting a structured service learning opportunity similar to our CAE project will continue to provide students with the benefit of being able to share knowledge with peers from across campus while removing the urgency of the process by offering more transparency and planning. The students were able to show knowledge in a variety of formats in the CAE project, showcasing their crafting skills, ability to interpret archeological research into a reproduction, and displaying and conveying knowledge visually and verbally. The learning was so strongly solidified for the students in this process that I want to give them this opportunity again.

Incorporating work from other classes that has proven successful, I would like to add the inclusive practice of access need check-ins to our classroom routine. I first learned it from Nicole Brewer at an anti-racist theatre training, but it has roots in disability justice. It has proven beneficial in other classes and has allowed students and myself to be more fully present by destigmatizing needs, recognizing that needs shift from day to day, and prioritizing healthy spaces.

I'd like to expand the assessment model into the final research project as much of that modeling was carried over from previous classes. I still think the scaffolded structure works well, but I want to be more inviting of practice as research and to bring it into alignment with our conversational assessment model more fully. I think by creating a reflective moment at each stage, we can dialogue about the current success of the work and where the student wants to put their energy next. I have learned from other classes, now that I have expanded the usage of the conversational assessment model, that some students have difficulty reflecting in writing, so I would like to offer both oral and written options for reflection to be more inclusive and to really get at the meat of reflection, which will help shape the next steps well.

Students asked for more quiz opportunities to test their knowledge, so I would like to offer these as self-test opportunities or low-stakes assessments that can help students evaluate their progress. I'd like to continue to offer the essay-style, choose-your-own-adventure options but also offer some ways for students to test their own goals. For instance, if a student wants to be able to quickly identify items visually by connecting names to images, I want them to have some opportunities to challenge themselves on this. I plan to create a small bank of quizzes as options and also show students some best practices for setting up self-tests specific to their goals and methods of learning to empower them to track their own progress.

Students tailored their note-taking strategies to their goals during the course, but some of the students struggled to comprehend this practice. I can offer some direct examples and also work with the class to brainstorm how to apply each goal to a variety of learning opportunities like note taking, summarizing, self-tests, picking a research topic, etc. By offering transparent application of the technique, I think more students will have the benefits that some of my students had the last time around. For example, one student wanted to learn terminology and so created a spreadsheet approach that created flashcards while another was interested in larger questions of historical context and structured notes around political movements and power structures.

I am excited about the successes I saw with the students and am eager to see how our next group of students makes this content their own. The addition of graduate students offers an opportunity to expand in both theory and practice and build relationships with the local community through a project they can help support with their research. These options for realized application of knowledge as they are learning research methods have great potential for students of all levels.

Notes

1 Boal, A., & McBride, C. A. *Theatre of the Oppressed* (Tcg ed.), Theatre Communications Group, 1993.
2 Freire, P., & Macedo, D. *Pedagogy of the Oppressed: 50th Anniversary Edition* (4th ed.), Bloomsbury Academic, 2018.
3 hooks, b. *Teaching to Transgress: Education as the Practice of Freedom*, Routledge, 1994.
4 Blum, Susan D., & Kohn, Alfie. *Ungrading: Why Rating Students Undermines Learning (and What to Do Instead)*, West Virginia University Press, 2020.
5 Tortora, K., & Marcketti, P. G. *Survey of Historic Costume: A History of Western Dress* (7th ed.), Fairchild Books, 2021.
6 Tortora, K., & Marcketti, P. G. *Survey of Historic Costume: A History of Western Dress* (7th ed.), Fairchild Books, 2021.

7 Anawalt, Patricia Rieff. *The Worldwide History of Dress*, Thames & Hudson, 2007.
8 Harvey, Sara M. "Persian Clothing." In J. Condra (Ed.), *The Greenwood Encyclopedia of Clothing through World History*, Greenwood Press, 2008.
9 Fashion and Race Database (currently behind a paywall).
10 Mark, J. J. "Cosmetics, Perfume, & Hygiene in Ancient Egypt." *World History Encyclopedia,* 2017, www.worldhistory.org/article/1061/cosmetics-perfume--hygiene-in-ancient-egypt/.
11 Adhikari, Saugat. *Top 10 Inventions and Discoveries of Persian Civilization*. Retrieved August 21, 2022, from ancienthistorylists.com, www.ancienthistorylists.com/mesopotamia-history/top-10-inventions-of-persian-civilizations/.
12 Chen, Heather. *This Designer Wore a Far-Right Paramilitary Outfit to Paris Fashion Week*. Retrieved January 26, 2022, from vice.com, www.vice.com/en/article/bvndma/arnold-putra-paris-fashion-week-far-right-pancasila-pemuda-youth.
13 Sorensen-Unruh, C. "A Stem Ungrading Case Study: A Reflection on First-Time Implementation in Organic Chemistry II." In S. D. Blum (Ed.), *Ungrading: Why Rating Students Undermines Learning (and What to Do Instead)*, West Virginia University Press, 2020.

9

Expanding and Deconstructing the Western Fashion History Ideology

Rafael Jaen

Course Description

The course studies context-specific dress codes from around the globe and the USA, and it is divided into four parts: Human Geography and Guilds, Festive Spirit and Heritage, Reenactment and Living History, and Costume Play and Gender Culture. Following the research of Dr. Pravina Shukla, associate professor of folklore and ethnomusicology at Indiana University Bloomington, students explore how the mobility of people, ideas, and practices across a variety of borders reflects on the choice of dress as a contemporary social experience under globalization. Part 1 addresses Southwestern Africa's Yoruba clothing and textile guilds that serve historical and environmental purposes. In Part 2, students study samba costumes in Brazil, their African religious roots, and urban integration. Part 3 explores New England's pre-Revolutionary War contexts and the value of historical reenactment and cultural representation in "living museums." Finally, Part 4 looks at the cosplay subculture, avatar embodiment, and gender expression through dress.

School: University of Massachusetts, Boston
Department: Performing Arts, Humanities, and Diversity Distribution
Course: Enlivening Cultural and Gender Identities Through Dress
Student Level/Description: Undergraduate theatre majors and non-majors
Class Size: 16
Hours/Week: Twice a week, 1.25 hours. each

Format: In person or remote synchronous

Text or Core Materials: Chapters and excerpts from the following books:

Beckwith, Carol and Fisher, Angela. *African Ceremonies: The Concise Edition*, Special ed., Harry N. Abrams, 2022.

Chuang, Ejen. *Cosplay in America: Volume 2*, Ejen Chuang, 2010.

George, Terry. *Carnival in Rio: Samba Samba Samba!* Earbooks, 2005.

Shapera, Anne-Elizabeth. *Easy Street: A Guide for Players in Improvised Interactive Environmental Performance, Walkaround Entertainment, and First-Person Historical Interpretation*, First ed., Lulu.com, 2012.

Shukla, Pravina. *Costume: Performing Identities Through Dress*, Indiana University Press, 2015.

Benson, Gifty, curator. *Wandering Spirit: African Wax Prints*, Exhibit USA, a National Division of Mid-America Arts Alliance Nebraska Arts Council and the National Endowment for the Arts, 2016.

Note: Additional journal articles, videos, and research websites will be posted on Blackboard.

Types of Access Needed: Books and journal articles are available at the library reserves, and video links, etc., are provided via Blackboard.

Additional Class Readings

"10 Traditional Brazilian Dances." https://theculturetrip.com/south-america/brazil/articles/10-traditional-brazilian-dances-you-should-know-about/

"Bantu Languages." https://www.britannica.com/art/Bantu-languages

"Batik in Africa." https://www.batikguild.org.uk/batik/history-of-batik/africa

Boston Tea Party. https://www.history.com/topics/american-revolution/boston-tea-party

Hansen, Jessica Champagne. "Theatre Artist by Day, Cosplayer by Night." *TD&T Journal* 54, Winter 2018, www.nxtbook.com/nxtbooks/hickmanbrady/tdt_2018winter/index.php#/38

Peirson-Smith, Anne. "Fashioning the Fantastical Self: An Examination of the Cosplay Dress-up Phenomenon in Southeast Asia." https://www.academia.edu/8085201/Fashioning_the_Fantastical_Self_An_Examination_of_the_Cosplay_Dress-up_Phenomenon_in_Southeast_Asia?email_work_card=title

Reyson, Stephen. "'Coming Out' as an Anime Fan: Cosplayers in the Anime Fandom, Fan Disclosure, and Well-Being." https://www.academia.edu/37241621/_Coming_out_as_an_anime_fan_Cosplayers_in_the_anime_fandom_fan_disclosure_and_well-being

Reyson, Stephen. "'Who I Want to Be': Self-Perception and Cosplayers' Identification with Their Favorite Characters." https://www.academia.edu/36169585/_Who_I_want_to_Be_Self-Perception_and_Cosplayers_Identification_with_their_Favorite_Characters

"South America: Human Geography." National Geographic Resource Library, https://www.nationalgeographic.org/encyclopedia/south-america-human-geography/

"Top 29 Historic Battle Reenactments." https://www.thehistorylist.com/travel/top-26-historic-battle-reenactments-thisyear

Reasons to Evolve

Today's classroom is an immersive learning lab where participants must acquire multiple skills leading to critical thinking and outside-the-box creativity. Such an environment challenges them to apply practices that depend on building relationships, acknowledging the relevance of studying and deconstructing the prevalent systems in our communities and networks. Additionally, since not all students in liberal arts courses are performing arts majors, teachers must provide communication agreements to support effective and inclusive discussions. For example, when looking at historical images, instructors and students must explore the value of comparative historical research by listening to diverse voices and points of view that celebrate cultural traditions and avoid appropriation or perceptual biases. Thus, the teaching expertise becomes a shared research topic, and the students become an ensemble. They can co-lead, be team players, and become the collective brain that offers rich and diverse artistic answers to topical subject matters.

Students enrolled in Enlivening Cultural and Gender Identities Through Dress study context-specific dress codes from the USA and around the globe. The subject of the course highlights an important aspect of global diversity: Looking at transnational notions of identity through dress codes in the context of human geography or "the study of the interrelationships between people, place and environment and how these vary spatially and temporally across and between locations" (2). In this course, that interrelation is expressed through the understanding that costume is "special dress that enables the expression of extraordinary identity in exceptional circumstances" (Shukla). Each ethnography-based case study will show how costumes are self-consciously and purposefully employed to express fundamental human needs: For sociability and creativity, historical and ethnic identity, class aspirations and gender. Finally, following a scaffolding process from teaching theory to practicing immersive skills via creative exercises, participants can build empathy and develop a sense of agency to face a world that expects them to be knowledgeable multi-hyphenates.

Enlivening Cultural and Gender Identities Through Dress was inspired by a call to submit humanities proposals funded by the Mellon Foundation at UMass Boston. The course idea grew out of rejecting traditional Western-heavy fashion history books that lend themselves to a linear teaching process that omits many events that influence world cultures. And thus, this class's main objective is to provide a place to examine and celebrate world cultures in a global/transnational system manifesting through time and without denying their otherness. In such space, students can ask questions that allow using research as an exploration tool to access different viewpoints. Contextualizing gender identities, fashion silhouettes, color theory, textiles manufacturing, etc. within a historical time frame and world hemisphere will highlight cultural connections and promote enlivened discussions. Today's classroom can be an exploration hub allowing the participation of diverse voices when defining the meaning of fashion and how we dress by using frameworks that include deconstructing systemic biases by allowing more authentic storytelling by unpacking traditions such as carnival pageantry and historical reenactment. Adding hands-on and creative interactive activities can also enable community building and play.

At UMass Boston, Enlivening Cultural and Gender Identities Through Dress provides a space where students can experience the diversity in the UMass Boston minority-majority community (and the greater Boston area) by appreciating how different groups dress. Central components of the class include interacting with artists and community members and exploring various social expressions. For example, students design fabrics inspired by the adire guilds and cloth patterns worn by Yoruba people in Nigeria. They explore the universal symbolism behind their ancient alphabet system and how these textiles are commercialized today. They interact with samba school members living in Boston and decode their dress styles by geographical location and socio-economic status. They tour the Boston Tea Party Museum and see how reenactors use dress to tell curated stories in the context of a "living museum." They also explore the cosplay subculture, the appropriation of anime characters and avatars, and the crossing of gender preconceptions. Participants conduct research, debate specific readings, and develop verbal reasoning and critical thinking in the process. Students read textbook chapters and journal articles and watch TED Talks and other relevant videos. They interact with guest speakers from the community and with guest presenters from other states via Zoom or face to face. Additionally, the course assignments allow the students to connect content to their personal experiences in a critical manner.

Course Outcomes

Students will develop an appreciation of costume as an expression of extraordinary identity in exceptional circumstances.

Students will develop an understanding of "dress" in the context of human geography and the way culture and traditions migrate geographically and historically.

Students will learn to describe "how costumes are self-consciously and purposefully employed to express basic human needs: For sociability, creativity, historical identity, heritage, and personality."

Students will examine the making and wearing of costume as a personal worldview, describing how these might be influenced by membership in a particular culture or social class.

Students will learn to describe how costume relates to issues of ethnicity, nationality, gender identity, spiritual beliefs, and other matters related to "otherness."

Students will deepen their awareness of costume dress codes and relevant societal issues by further investigating cultural representation and appropriation.

Students will increase oral and written communication skills.

Students will develop critical thinking and leadership skills required for rigorous research, essay writing, and presentation of original ideas.

Students will participate in the creative act of "enlivening identities through dress" through questioning, creating, interacting, and presenting topics.

Table 9.1 Weekly Schedule

Week	Topic	Content Description	Assignment
1	Guilds and Human Geography, 15%	Southern Africa Bantu region textile guilds	Textbook and journal article readings, video comments, and class discussions
2		Research and application	Additional readings, experiential learning
3		Review	Class discussion and essay writing

Week	Topic	Content Description	Assignment
4	Festive Spirit and Heritage, 15%	Samba costumes in Brazil	Textbook and journal article readings, video comments, and class discussions
5		Spring Vacation	Spring Vacation
6		Research and application	Additional readings, experiential learning
7		Review	Class discussion and essay writing Final paper discussion
8	Reenactment and Living History, 15%	Historical reenactment: New England's pre-Revolutionary War contexts	Textbook and journal article readings, video comments, and class discussions
9		Research and application	Additional readings, experiential learning
10		Review	Class Discussion and Essay Writing
11	Costume Play and Culture, 15%	The cosplay subculture	Textbook and journal article readings, video comments, and class discussions
12		Research and application	Additional readings, experiential learning
13		Review	Class discussion and essay writing
14	Final Paper, 15%	Proposal discussion	Abstract and outline
15		Method	Revised outline and drafts
16		Presentation	Final presentation and TED Talk

Source: Rafael Jaen, 2022

Table 9.2 Assignment Details

Content Description	Assignments: Readings, Videos, Discussion, and Field
Human geography, Southwestern Africa Yoruba textile guilds	**Textbook and Journal Article Readings** Costume: *Performing Identities Through Dress*: Introduction and Chapter 1: "Festive Spirit" "Human Geography: Defining Human Geography." Research Guides, n.d. https://research guides.dartmouth.edu/human_geography. **Video Comments** *The Devil Wears Prada* movie excerpt: https://youtube.com/watch?v=Ja2fgquYTCg. Adichie, Chimamanda Ngozi. *The Danger of a Single Story*, TEDGlobal, 2009, https://youtu.be/D9Ihs241zeg. **Class Discussion** What are the relevant aspects of Shukla's approach? What is human geography? How does human geography relate to the way people dress? What role do guilds play in cultural globalization? What are the dangers of re-telling the "single story"?
Research and application	**Additional Readings** "Bantu Language," www.britannica.com/art/Bantu-languages "Batik in Africa," https://www.batikguild.org.uk/batik/history **Experiential Learning** Create a fabric class banner inspired by Yoruba textiles designed as a group.
Review	**Class Discussion and Essay Writing** Topics: Guilds and human geography What role do guilds play in globalization? What are the dangers of re-telling the "single story"?

Samba costumes in Brazil	**Textbook and Journal Article Readings** *Carnival in Rio: Samba*, Hardcover, September 2005, by Terry George "South America: Human Geography." *National Geographic Resource Library*, https://www.nationalgeographic.org/encyclopedia/south-america-human-geography/ **Video Comments** Shared in Class **Class Discussion** How did samba music come to be? How do schools of Samba build community and promote guilds? What are the main differences between schools of samba in New England, New York, and cities in Brazil? What are the topics covered by the lyrics, and how do they translate to dress?
Research and application	**Additional Readings** *Costume: Performing Identities Through Dress*: Chapter 2: "Heritage" "10 Traditional Brazilian Dances," https://theculturetrip.com/south-america/brazil/articles/10-traditional-brazilian-dances-you-should-know-about/ **Experiential Learning** Conversations with and show and tell and dance demo by members of the Samba Viva Dance Music and Ensemble during class.
Review	**Class Discussion and Essay Writing** Topic: Carnival pageantries and religion What other carnival pageantries have religious origins? Why do people assemble and produce carnival competitions and parades?

(*Continued*)

Table 9.2 Continued

Content Description	Assignments: Readings, Videos, Discussion, and Field
Historical reenactment: New England's pre-Revolutionary War contexts	**Textbook and Journal Article Readings** Costume: Performing Identities Through Dress: Chapter 5: "Living History" Daugbjerg, Mads. "Re-enactment and Engagement" www.academia.edu/35631707/Re-enactment_and_Engagement **Video Comments** Shared in class **Class Discussion** What is historical reenactment? How do communities find meaning in it?
Research and application	**Additional Readings** Boston Tea Party, www.history.com/topics/american-revolution/boston-tea-party **Experiential Learning** Visit the Tea Party Museum in Boston Harbor for a guided tour and conversation with Audrey Stuck-Girard, reenactor, fashion historian, and costume maker for the museum. Engage in conversation with Dr. Adrienne J. Keene, an American and Native American scholar, writer, and activist, via her *Native Appropriations* blog. How do we make sure we're not appropriating history or misrepresenting it?
Review	**Class Discussion and Essay Writing** Historical reenactment and cultural appropriation What is historical reenactment? How do communities find meaning through it? What are other similar areas in which people do reenactments? What is living history; is it theatre? How do we make sure we are not appropriating history or misrepresenting it?

The cosplay subculture	**Textbook and Journal Article Readings** *Costume: Performing Identities Through Dress*: Conclusion: "Costume as Elective Identity" *Cosplay in America*: Essays by Andrea Letamendi and Liz Ohanesian Peirson-Smith, Anne. "Fashioning the Fantastical Self: An Examination of the Cosplay Dress-up Phenomenon in Southeast Asia," www.academia.edu/8085201/Fashioning_the_Fantastical_Self_An_Examination_of_the_Cosplay_Dress-Up_Phenomenon_in_Southeast_Asia?email_work_card=title **Video Comments** Review videos at "Cosplay in America," www.youtube.com/channel/UCiZb0_Yb4YZiFs9uuRmGxIA **Class Discussion** What relevant aspects of Shukla's approach connect to cosplay? How does cosplay manifest as a gender self-expression? What are the cultural assumptions about cosplay in the Western and Eastern Hemispheres?
Research and Application	**Additional Readings** "Theatre Artist by Day, Cosplayer by Night," by Jessica Champagne Hanson "'Coming Out' as an Anime Fam: Cosplayers in the Anime Fandom, Fan Disclosure, and Well-Being," by Stephen Reysen "Who I Want to Be: Self-Perception and Cosplayers' Identification with Their Favorite Characters" by Stephen Reysen **Experiential Learning** Class discussion via Zoom or Skype with Jessica Champagne Hanson
Review	**Class Discussion and Essay Writing** Topics: Cosplay and gender, cosplay as art Why do we dismiss the cosplay world?

(*Continued*)

Table 9.2 Continued

Content Description	Assignments: Readings, Videos, Discussion, and Field
Proposal Discussion	**Abstract and Outline** Discuss topics during class in groups referring to the "Final Paper Notes" section in the syllabus. Present abstract, outline, and writing plan to the class.
Method	**Revised Outline and Drafts** Upload the draft to the online learning platform. Discuss draft revisions during class. Fine tune research.
Presentation	**Final Paper Presentations and TED Talk** Upload the final paper to the online learning platform. Present a short summary to the class as a mini TED Talk.

Source: Rafael Jaen, 2022

Sample Assignment

The course's Part 1 focuses on human geography and guilds, emphasizing the interrelationships between people, place, and environment. Homework includes watching videos and TED Talks that help guide the in-class discussions. In addition to writing comments on Blackboard, students join groups and create textiles inspired by what they learn about Southwestern Africa's Yoruba clothing and the adire – tied and dyed – textile guilds. The symbology includes (global) concerns of Yoruba life ranging from nature to religion, philosophy, everyday life, and seminal events.

In *The Devil Wears Prada*'s iconic "cerulean monologue," fashion editor Miranda Priestly (played by actress Meryl Streep) chides her new intern, Andrea (played by Anne Hathaway), after she refers to design clothing as "stuff" during runway season preparations. In response, editor Priestly describes the specificity of the color "cerulean" in under three minutes. While styling a runway outfit, she covers the color's history from haute couture to department stores, and she also acknowledges the fashion industry's countless jobs unseen by consumers. In the end, she instructs Andrea that she is wearing a (cerulean) "sweater that was selected for [her] by the people in the [fashion editor's] room . . . From a pile of 'stuff!'"[1] This monologue relates to "design clothing" in the context of human geography or "the study of the interrelationships between people, place, and environment, and how these vary spatially and temporally across and between locations."[2] In this course, such interrelation expresses through the understanding that costume is special dress that enables the expression of extraordinary identity in exceptional circumstances (Shukla). Each ethnography-based case study will show how costumes are self-consciously and purposefully employed to express fundamental human needs: For sociability and creativity, historical and ethnic identity, class aspirations, and gender.

Since Part 1 also addresses the "single story," confronting biased ideas that we may have about the people in different regions of the African continent, students must watch and comment on a second video: *The Danger of a Single Story*. In it, novelist Chimamanda Adichie tells the story of how she found her authentic cultural voice and warns that "if we hear only a single story about another person or country, we risk a critical misunderstanding." A "[single story] robs people of their dignity; it makes our recognition of our equal humanity difficult. It emphasizes how we are different rather than how we are similar."[3,4] The video addresses the underlying themes of implicit biases and power structures across cultures. In this context, *Dress* becomes a critical way to claim self-identity and global citizenship.

Experiential Learning

For this assignment, students identify words and images representing their beliefs, ancestry, or ethnicity to explore the human geography idea of interrelationships between people and places in the class environment. Then, they present them as "motifs" in class, asking for feedback from other students, discussing their significance, and unpacking biases or misconceptions. Afterward, they abstract these motifs and collaborate with their classmates to create human geography banners for painting or printing on fabric. Finally, writing an essay will allow students to reflect, journal, and further research aspects that influence how they see themselves in their network and how they dress.

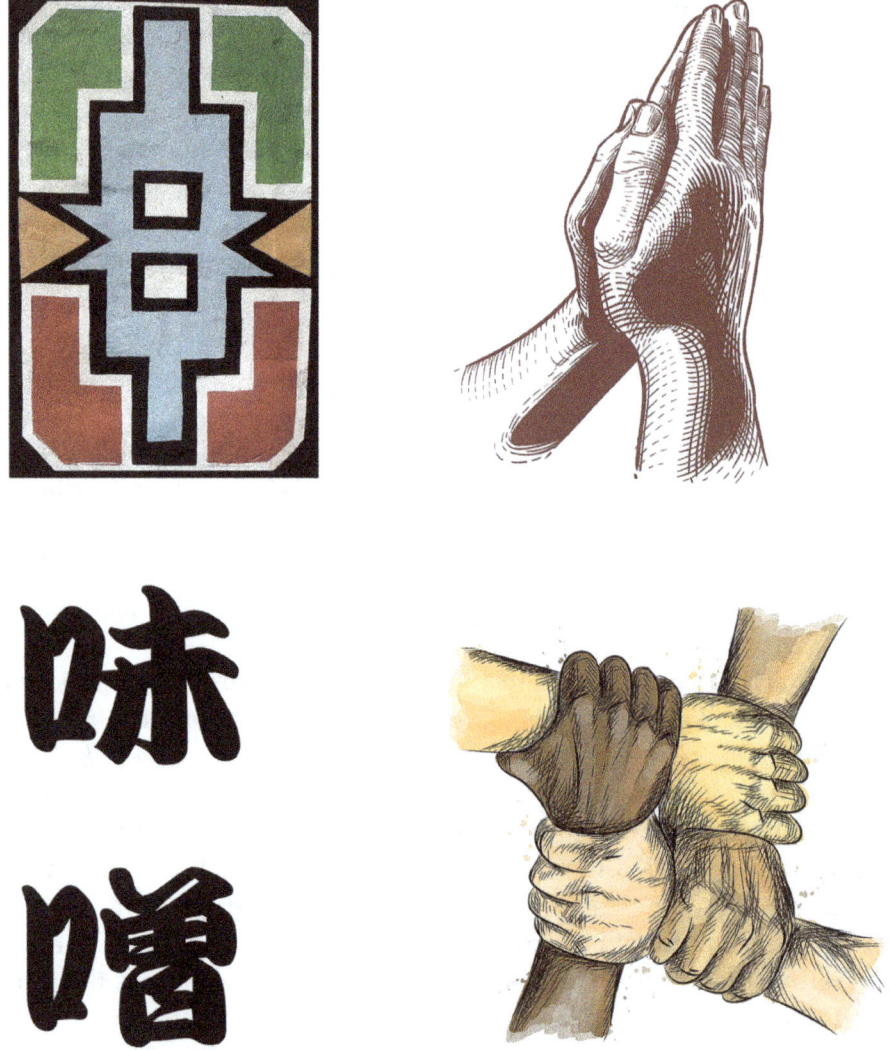

Figure 9.1 Student images for class banner, 2021: Image of praying hands, four hands forming a square, a geometric square image, and two Asian characters

In one of the classes, students presented words and motifs such as "Cradle of Humankind," "Bendiciones," "Comfort," and "United" (See Figures 9.1-9.3) and during class discussions, the group learned the meaning behind each symbol. The "Cradle of Humankind" motif represents traditional Ndebele-painted walls at Lesedi Cultural Village, Cradle of Humankind, South Africa. The application of wall decoration usually indicates times of transition in a woman's life.[5] "Bendiciones" refers to blessing hands united for prayer.[6] The "Comfort" image is miso in Japanese calligraphy. Miso is a fermented seasoning essential to the everyday diet of Japanese people, and the motif symbolizes the nostalgic comfort and warmth of miso soup.[7]

Figure 9.2 Student multicolor printed banner, 2021: Images have been organized into a gridded pattern

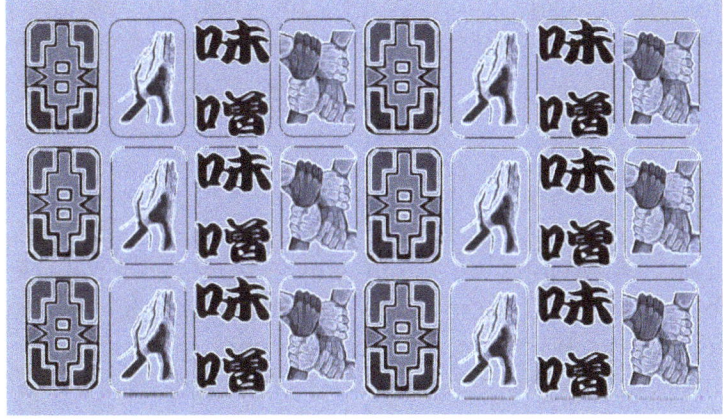

Figure 9.3 Student adire indigo banner, 2021: Images have been aligned in a gridded pattern in a monochromatic color palette

"United" represents a group of young and diverse people holding hands and expressing positive teamwork concepts. It also means family overseas and a connection to heritage.[8]

Reflections

We refer to colleagues with long careers as mature or seasoned theatre design and technology artists, and while it is a compliment, such descriptions suggest an ending. In my case, I am a seasoned practitioner, a life-long learner, and a self-professed multi-hyphenate, constantly developing my artistic expression. Costume design, research, and manufacturing are passions that have led my teaching. Teaching, in turn, has led to writing. I love how these three elements inform each other, igniting my curiosity as an artist, educator, and scholar. But the most significant skill we have as designers and teachers is the ability to listen.

Being a mentor in a classroom where students' listening can help them harmonize and complement each other is a privilege. And thus, over time, my classrooms have become immersive learning labs where participants acquire multiple skills, becoming part of an ensemble. For example, when analyzing a script or looking at historical images, students explore the value of comparative historical research to produce designs that celebrate cultural traditions and avoid appropriation or promoting perceptual biases. Given the influx of information on the internet and how readily available misinformation has become, listening, asking questions, and unpacking topics respectfully can help us pivot (when needed) to achieve course objectives beyond expectations. Such listening requires a new kind of endurance: Empathy, patience, and flexibility.

I look forward to enabling future learning spaces where students embody art that promotes empathy, visibility, and celebration of their individual stories. I am also excited to observe how they reinvent the idea of being a seasoned artist while elevating cultural traditions and creating meaningful storytelling.

Notes

1 "Watchmen, Dr. Manhattan Comments." *Monologue*, n.d., www.monologuedb.com/comedic-female-monologues/the-devil-wears-prada-miranda-priestly/, www.youtube.com/watch?v=Ja2fgquYTCg.
2 "Human Geography: Defining Human Geography." *Research Guides*, n.d., https://researchguides.dartmouth.edu/human_geography.

3 "Wandering Spirit: African Wax Prints." *Mid-America Arts Alliance*, n.d., https://eusa.org/exhibition/wandering-spirit-african-wax- prints/.
4 Adiche, Chimamanda Ngozi. *The Danger of A Single Story*, TEDGlobal, 2009, https://youtu.be/D9Ihs241zeg.
5 Alami Image License ID WAERD1 for magazines and books.
6 Alami Image License ID 2B09KYC for all media in perpetuity.
7 Alami Image License ID G04W5 for magazines and books.
8 Alami Image License ID PXBKJY for all media in perpetuity.

10

Fashion and Costume

Global Adornment and Attire

Sarah M. Oliver

Course Description

There were three main goals that I always felt were important when developing this course. I felt it was essential to develop a non-Western costume course that could be an optional three-credit course taught alongside a Eurocentric costume history offering. In full recognition that many other institutions or departments might not have the room to support an additional three credits in already over-full curriculums, I decided to build the course grouped into "big ideas" or modules that would allow a module to be "lifted" and inserted into a more traditional Eurocentric costume history survey course. The use of modules would hopefully allow exposure to historical or traditional dress of each country, with less regard to specific time or period.

I developed the course so it would be approved for my university's race and ethnicity requirement to increase enrollment university-wide since this course would not be required in my department. With this course, I wanted to encourage critical connections between the global history of clothing, theories of race and ethnicity, and the interconnected nature of diversity in adornment and dress. Global fashion was considered with an emphasis on exposure to quintessential historical or traditional dress and how historic costume informs the global fashion industry. Consequently, I viewed this class as a "sampling" of culture and costume not usually included in the traditional Western costume history course.

> School: University of Michigan
>
> Department: Theatre and Drama, Design and Production, School of Music, Theatre, and Dance
>
> Student Level/Description: BFA design and production specialization, general undergraduate
>
> Class Size: Designed for 15–25 students; next cohorts will be 150 as the course is approved for the university-wide race and ethnicity requirement
>
> Hours/Week: 3 credit hours
>
> Format: Synchronous in person
>
> Text or Core Materials: The required text for this course is *The Worldwide History of Dress*, by Patricia Reiff Anawalt, ISBN: 9780500513637, but the book is currently out of print. It is an excellent resource, and I have hope it will be reprinted. In addition, a variety of supplemental handouts, selected readings, guest lecturers, and instructor-generated lectures are utilized.
>
> Types of Access Needed: All course materials are available to students via Canvas. Students are required to have electronic devices that can access the internet. Learning platforms used: Google Suite, Padlet, Zoom, and Thinglink.

I did not have a lightning bolt moment that caused a radical change to my current methods of teaching costume history; rather, changes came about at a slow and steady pace in my costume history courses over the last 10 years. The first inklings that I might need to adjust really began when I was teaching a Western costume history course in Hong Kong to a population of students who had little to no background in Western history. I discovered most of the connections to significant historical events, people, or industrial improvements that I usually had in common with my students were not in these students' lexicons. By necessity, over the semester and the intervening few years, my Western costume history course became more global, and I found that it was easier for the students to identify with historical fashion and dress when paired directly with the 20th century designers and fashion they were currently consuming. The structure of the course began to move away from a "parade of fashion" approach, and I started introducing weekly historical research projects that asked the students to compare and then contrast a historical garment to a modern-day fashion garment.

During the same timeframe when I was teaching students in Hong Kong, I was also teaching an online costume history course to master's-level students in the United States. Even though I was teaching from what I think of now as the standard "parade of fashion" method that I had been taught in school, my late-night Skype classes were often interrupted by students who were hungry for the kind of engagement with global dress and fashion I was exploring daily while living overseas. I was eager to provide my students with opportunities to engage with clothing and dress outside continental Europe and find ways to connect 20th-century fashion in a more direct manner than I was currently testing out in my classes in Hong Kong.

As I write this chapter now, most instructors and professors have engaged with online teaching, whether by choice or by necessity during the COVID-19 pandemic. Whatever your personal feelings about the pedagogical implications of utilizing a Zoom or asynchronous class for instruction, if you are still in the teaching profession at this point, you have almost certainly done so. But in 2012, teaching costume history via Skype from Hong Kong to students in the US at 3:00 a.m. twice a week was the new frontier. I didn't have tools like Zoom, Kaltura, or Lecture Capture, and it certainly wasn't a smooth operation every week teaching online, but I did begin to understand the potential power of "walking" students through costume collections and museum exhibitions from many different countries so they could explore global fashion without leaving the United States. I began to feel for the first time that I had a way to both amass a wealth of information about global fashion that could be captured for students to consume and connect students one on one with costume experts in various countries without the expense of flying them to the United States.

As I considered how I would develop a new global fashion course to teach when I returned to the United States, I wanted to incorporate online platforms and methods of exploring content online together into course assignments. It was important that I explore course assignments that asked the student to participate in different roles through which they were currently consuming fashion and costume media, such as an Instagram blogger, style influencer, museum curator, or content creator. Following the fashion industry, I became hyper aware of these types of media as leading voices in promoting racial justice, diversity, and body positivity and wanted to connect lectures to media students currently consume, reinforcing how marginalized groups are challenging the privilege of who is telling the story and rethinking race, ethnicity, culture, and religion.

I also began to give serious consideration to where in the semester I was introducing any global fashion and began to evaluate how long I was spending on ancient Greek, Roman, Minoan, and Babylonian dress compared to the mad rush at the end of the semester to squeeze in any information about

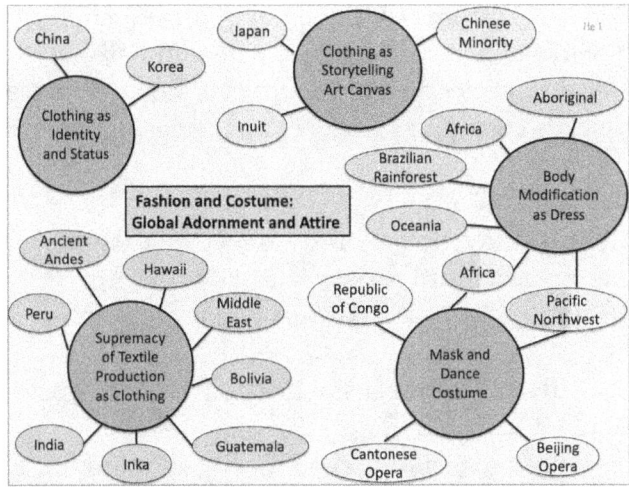

Figure 10.1 Mind map of five course modules
Source: Sarah M. Oliver, 2021

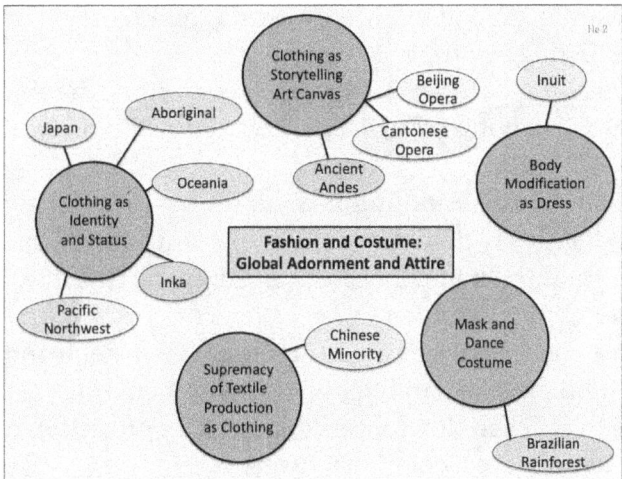

Figure 10.2 Example of student final project to reassign 10 countries/cultures to course modules
Source: Madelyn Domagala, 2021

costume and dress after 1990. I felt that every day that went by, the sheer volume of information on costume and dress was multiplying, and what needed to be taught in costume history class meant that I could not conceive of situating a global costume module within my current Western costume history course. I felt it was essential to develop a non-Western costume course that could be an optional three credit course taught alongside a Eurocentric costume history course within the curriculum. Most of all, I wanted to offer a course in fashion and costume that offered an introduction to the core theoretical foundations of critical race studies, with emphases on historical dress, global fashion, and intersectional approaches to how we present our bodies and fashion, which is changing rapidly in an increasingly diverse world.

Course Objectives
- Students will study globally interconnected costume history articles, garments, artifacts, and books;
- Students will gain a broad but accurate recognition of non-Western costume;
- Students will analyze the aesthetic and practical aspects of global dress; and
- Students will engage and think critically about topics such as power, inequality, race, ethnicity, and racism as they relate to global fashion and costume.

Learning Outcomes
- Demonstrate a broad but accurate recognition of non-Western costume, utilizing appropriate vocabulary;
- When viewing garments, artifacts, and costume, be able to identify countries of origin and to list the characteristics on which this identification was based;
- Understand origins and implications of race, ethnicity, and identity in an increasingly diverse world in the context of global fashion and costume and the interconnected nature of the diversity in culture and dress.
- Generate significant questions about global fashion and costume history and develop strategies to answer them.
- Be able to practice close observation and appreciation of the aesthetic and practical aspects of global dress.

Building the Bones
The creation of this course had three distinct phases:

Dreaming and content collection
Workshop and development of the course design
Module creation and sequencing

When I first conceived of this course, the integration of online resources was significantly more limited than it is now, and high-quality information about global dress and costume was generally restricted to the purview of

Table 10.1 Syllabus Calendar

Week	Module	Reading Assignment	Lecture	Assignment
Week 1	**Clothing as Identity and Status** (China and Korea)	McFeeters, Stephanie. "Counter Protesters Join Kimono Fray at MFA." *Boston Globe*, July 18 2015. Qin, Amy. "Teenager's Prom Dress Stirs Furor in U.S. – but Not in China." *ProQuest*, May 2, 2018.	Introduction to Global Fashion	Cultural appropriation reading and Has Your Opinion Changed? discussion.
Week 2	**Clothing as Identity and Status** (China and Korea)	Anawalt, Patricia Rieff. *The Worldwide History of Dress*, Thames & Hudson Inc. 2007, 153–173. Tely, Fung Wing (Producer) and Tang Yuen, M.J. (Director). *Chinese Foot Binding: The Vanishing Lotus*, 2004. [Video/DVD]	Rank and Status in Qing Dynasty Costume Korea, the Land of Hat	Foot Binding and Body modification in Western fashion
Week 3	**Clothing as Identity and Status** (China and Korea)	Anawalt, Patricia Rieff, *The Worldwide History of Dress*, Thames & Hudson Inc. 2007, 180–193.	Chinese Costume History Highlights The Development of the Qipao	12 Imperial Symbols of the Bat Pao

(*Continued*)

Table 10.1 Continued

Week	Module	Reading Assignment	Lecture	Assignment
Week 4	**Clothing as Storytelling Art Canvas** (Japan, Chinese minority, Inuit)	English, Bonnie, *Japanese Fashion Designers: The Work and Influence of Issey Miyake, Yohji Yamamoto and Rei Kawakubo*, Berg, 2011, 1–7.	Kimono as Art Canvas. Japanese Boro Clothing Happi and Hanten Coats	20th-century Japanese designers and makers
Week 5	**Clothing as Storytelling Art Canvas** (Japan, Chinese minority, Inuit)	Anawalt, Patricia Rieff. *The Worldwide History of Dress*, Thames & Hudson Inc. 2007, 176–179.	Chinese Minority Storytelling Through Textile Ainu Textiles and History of Yukata	Independent Research Blog, Miao textile production
Week 6	**Clothing as Storytelling Art Canvas** (Japan, Chinese Minority, Inuit)	Smithsonian Arctic Studies Center in Alaska. *Smithsonian Learning Lab Collection: Conversations: Challenges to Inuit Art Sovereignty*, Smithsonian Learning Lab, Smithsonian Office of Educational Technology, October 20, 2021, https://learninglab.si.edu/q/ll-c/Clw3cYbEU4OHtTQJ. Anawalt, Patricia Rieff. *The Worldwide History of Dress*, Thames & Hudson Inc. 2007, 334–345.	Inuit Clothing Production Pacific Northwest Costume and Weaving	Pacific Northwest Adornment Museum curation project

Week 7	**Body Modification as Dress** (Brazilian rainforest, Africa, Aboriginal, Oceania, and Pacific Northwest)	Mokoena, Hlonipha. *Slavery to Colonialism and School Rules: A History of Myths About Black Hair*, August 31, 2016, https://theconversation.com/from-slavery-to-colonialism-and-school-rules-a-history-of-myths-about-black-hair-64676.	No Clothing Equals Dressed – Body Adornment in Africa	African hairstyle blog post based on reading
Week 8	**Body Modification as Dress** (Brazilian rainforest, Africa, Aboriginal, Oceania, and Pacific Northwest)	"Scarification." *Pitt Rivers Virtual Collections*, 2021, http://web.prm.ox.ac.uk/bodyarts/index.php/permanent-body-arts/scarification.html. United Nations Declaration on the Rights of Indigenous Peoples (articles 11, 12, 13, and 31), www.un.org/development/desa/indigenouspeoples/wpcontent/uploads/sites/19/2018/11/UNDRIP_E_web.pdf.	Body Marking to Mark Stages in Life	Decolonizing museums assignment

(*Continued*)

Table 10.1 Continued

Week	Module	Reading Assignment	Lecture	Assignment
Week 9	**Body Modification as Dress** (Brazilian rainforest, Africa, Aboriginal, Oceania, and Pacific Northwest)	Nuwer, Rachel. "Anthropology: The Sad Truth About Uncontacted Tribes." BBC, August 3, 2014, https://www.bbc.com/future/article/20140804-sad-truth-of-uncontacted-tribes	Dress and Adornment in Oceania Feathers and Body Paint in the Brazilian Rainforest	Body modification as dress
Week 10	**Supremacy of Textile Production as Clothing** (Ancient Andes, Hawaii, Middle East, Inka, Peru, Bolivia, Guatemala, Ghana)	Anawalt, Patricia Rieff. *The Worldwide History of Dress*, Thames & Hudson Inc. 2007, 550–561.	Weaving Is the Thing: Cloth and Dress in Andes and Guatemala	Kuba velvet blog post
Week 11	**Supremacy of Textile Production as Clothing** (Ancient Andes, Hawaii, Middle East, Inka, Peru, Bolivia, Guatemala, Ghana)	Anawalt, Patricia Rieff. *The Worldwide History of Dress*, Thames & Hudson Inc. 2007, 312–331.	The Feather as Textile and Clothing	Modern feather textile artist blog post

Week 12	**Supremacy of Textile Production as Clothing** (Ancient Andes, Hawaii, Middle East, Inka, Peru, Bolivia, Guatemala, Ghana)	Anawalt, Patricia Rieff. *The Worldwide History of Dress*, Thames & Hudson Inc. 2007, 226–236.	Draped Clothing; No Sewing Required. Footwear in India	Diwali fashion assignment
Week 13	**Mask and Dance Costume** (Africa, Nigeria, and Chinese opera costume)	Tian, Min. "Male Dan: The Paradox of Sex, Acting, and Perception of Female Impersonation in Traditional Chinese Theatre." *Asian Theatre Journal* 17, no. 1, University of Hawai'i Press, 2000, 78–97, doi:10.1353/atj.2000.0007	Beijing Opera Theatre and Costume Cantonese Opera Theatre and Costume	Beijing Opera facial makeup assignment
Week 14	**Mask and Dance Costume** (Africa, Nigeria, and Chinese opera costume)	Anawalt, Patricia Rieff. *The Worldwide History of Dress*, Thames & Hudson Inc. 2007, 527–549.	The Power of the Mask and Dance	Final mind map project

Source: Sarah M. Oliver, 2021

the library if you lived in the United States. Because the process of creating this course has been a slow and steady one over the last 10-plus years, in full transparency, I began in a manner that is probably not as valid anymore due to the fast and furious advancements in online information and technology brought on by the COVID-19 pandemic.

I was living and working internationally 10 years ago, which was a great benefit to gathering content for this pre-pandemic course. Once I knew I wanted to devise a non-Western costume history course that could be an optional three-credit course taught alongside a Eurocentric costume history offering, I evaluated which countries I felt I had in-depth knowledge of costume and dress of. I then identified a list of countries I felt warranted more research before I would consider adding them to my course. I began writing grants funded through my institution for international travel to visit museums, see exhibitions, and work with experts in the countries that I had identified as "deficient" in my personal knowledge base of global costume. At the time, I was living in Asia and was able to concentrate my travels in a large swath of countries in the Eastern Hemisphere within four to five hours flight time from where I lived.

In-person travel allowed me to sit at a loom beside artisans on tiny coral reef islands south of mainland Japan, weaving *bashofu* cloth for kimono in the same traditions that date back to the 13th century. I was able to work with museum curators in Hangzhou, China, at the China National Silk Museum to understand how the layers of undergarments fit against the body in historic Chinese clothing, which I would never have been able to truly understand by reading a book or looking at pictures online. Being backstage with the dressers for the Cantonese Opera, watching the artform of "tying on" headdress and costume is an unbelievable experience that I am now able to bring into my classroom for my students. These are just a few examples of the original grant-funded trips that remain as cornerstone sections of my course today because of the richness and depth of material I was able to learn from my in-person travel.

The idea that one is required to travel to develop a course like this is, I believe, outdated now, with the explosion of high-quality information about global dress and fashion on the internet currently. The COVID-19 pandemic truly allowed museums and collections the space and time to create spectacular online collections that are highly searchable and user friendly. I feel the work we must do now is to curate and vet those online sources for our students and, hopefully, support the online information with experts in the field whenever possible. Zoom has opened the entire world to our students with the ability to invite international speakers into our classrooms as guests and experts on the subjects you might identify as your "deficient" areas. To travel, experience, and see global dress and costume firsthand is ideal, but I do not feel as I did 10 years ago when I wrote those grants and hopped on a plane to travel. High-quality information is now readily available online to impart to my students for a course like this.

The second phase involved course design and syllabus development. My Eurocentric costume history course was a class I had inherited, and I felt a sense of obligation to teach what I had been taught in the manner that I had learned it. However, with this new course, I felt a sense of liberation, a feeling that I could really begin from the ground up with no holdovers from the methods of the past, and I began to seek out resources and workshops that offered guidance on how to reinvent my methods.

Those first days and months of the lockdowns in the early pandemic gave me the availability and time to work with our university's Center for Research on Learning and Teaching (CRLT) on campus to revise my syllabus to serve as a learning device and guide for students in a way I had not had time for before. I began by taking several workshops offered by my institution on syllabus design and equity-focused assessment as well as attending the ReDressing the Narrative costume history pedagogy workshop led by Chloe Chapin and Christianne Myers of the American Theatrical Costume Association (ATCA) in May of 2020. This gave me a sense of community, invigorated my research in course development, and made me realize that other costume professionals were grappling with similar issues surrounding costume history pedagogy.

Amongst the various workshops and courses I participated in as research for the development of this course, one that was particularly meaningful was Leading Change: Go Beyond Gamification with Gameful Learning, an EdX massive open online course (MOOC) by Barry Fishman and Rachel Niemer. The key principles of gameful learning pedagogy are choice, feedback, freedom to fail, and building up points from zero. The key principles of gameful learning resonate clearly with the collaborative work we typically do in the theatre and the kinds of interactions that happen between designer and director and designer and maker. I set about designing my course so students had meaningful choices about assignments and multiple opportunities to submit work for feedback from both colleagues in the class and myself and created a grading system that started at 0 points with a transparent system for how to build up to a desired grade.

The final phase of the course design was determining that instead of teaching the class in a "parade of fashion" or linear history of each country, I would group countries or regions into five "big ideas" or modules. (See Figure 10.1.) The purpose of the modules was to allow for greater flexibility to make cross-cultural connections, with less regard to time or period. It would also allow for a bit of a "plug and play" in that first year or two while I was testing out the course and was not sure which countries I felt completely confident about the material or guest speaker for. The modules have evolved over the years, but I am currently teaching from these five categories: Clothing as identity and status, clothing as storytelling art canvas, body modification as dress, supremacy of textile production as clothing, and mask and dance costume. The development of these modules has also led to the creation of excellent lectures that can be "lifted" from my course and moved easily into my Western costume history course as needed.

> **One Brief Bit of Advice**
>
> If you are going to begin teaching a course in global costume history or incorporate significant sections of global fashion history into your current costume history course, you need to prepare yourself for "The Talk." And by "The Talk," I am speaking about how to address conversations surrounding cultural appropriation versus cultural appreciation. Fashion designers are finally beginning to acknowledge traditional cultural expressions (TCEs), but the list of fashion designers who have faced backlash for insensitive cultural appropriation in their collections is vast and long. The debate in your class surrounding appropriation versus appreciation will most likely be a nuanced one but will get to the heart of why you might be considering incorporating elements of global costume history into your course. My best advice is that you need to put in the research time while you are developing your course if you are not familiar with this issue and then prepare your students for how best to engage in conversations that center on appreciation before it turns into appropriation.

In 2021, our school made the decision to add a race and ethnicity (R/E) requirement to most undergraduate degrees. The criteria for inclusion in the pre-approved R/E courses require that they model and embody foundational changes in their respective fields and include substantial engagement with and discussion of the following four topics:

- The meanings of race, ethnicity, power, and racism;
- Racial and ethnic intolerance and resulting inequality;
- Comparisons of discrimination based on race, ethnicity, religion, social class, gender identity and/or gender expression, ability/disability status, sexual orientation, and national origin; and

Figure 10.3 Sample project: Objects from nature as body adornment and dress assignment

Source: Madelyn Domagala, 2021

- How the arts interact with and intervene in issues of racism, intolerance, prejudice, and discrimination as well as resistance and social change.

A Fashion and Costume: Global Adornment and Attire course seemed an ideal fit for this requirement and would potentially increase enrollment in my course from outside my department.

The application required an annotated syllabus, a course description and course objectives that included an explicit commitment to R/E educational goals, and a "student-facing statement" describing the intent of the R/E requirement. The exercise of annotating each weekly assignment was a deeply thought-provoking activity that led to a greater understanding and comprehension of how all the assignments in my course fit together with my lectures throughout the semester. The entire process, while very labor intensive, afforded me an overall perspective about the design of my course that I could not have appreciated without going through the process. It both expanded my understanding of what I was asking of my students and connected the dots for me with a very distinct throughline about how to engage with the work of people and artists who have been traditionally excluded from costume and dress.

Sample Project
(See Figures 10.4, 10.5.)

Chinese Ornaments of Imperial Bat Robe for Empress Cixi: A Modern Motif Design Interpretation

Assignment Objective
This assignment examines the symbols of the Qing Dynasty's imperial garments. The goal is for students to begin to understand the meaning and symbolism of the 12 Imperial symbols and the visual system of power and privilege embedded in these symbols. Once students have gained a basic fluency in decoding Chinese art's visual language, they are then asked to contextualize the traditional Chinese symbols and design concepts for a Lóng Páo that integrates cultural elements into a design of their own, creating a culturally responsive garment design.

Assignment Description
In our imaginary world for this project, the Chinese Imperial ruler of the Qing Dynasty is a female, Empress Cixi. She uses the bat as her Imperial animal and the centerpiece of all Imperial robes. Your assignment is to devise a "Bat Lóng Páo" that features not only the bat but also the 12 Imperial symbols that you decide Empress Cixi should have. As you have studied the 12 traditional Imperial symbols, you should use your newfound knowledge to create your own iconography and symbolism for the 12 Imperial symbols you choose for Empress Cixi's Bat Lóng Páo.

This project can utilize found images that are incorporated into your vision of Empress Cixi's Bat Lóng Páo or images that are drawn by you. Either approach is perfectly fine. What is important is that you use the Chinese symbolic meaning of imagery to justify your choice of each image. Remember that the placement of your Imperial symbols has significance and should be considered carefully.

Each finished project should detail the overall design for a Bat Lóng Páo.

- The bat as the central animal featured on the front and back of your Bat Lóng Páo (worth 50 points);
- A visual image of each symbol, either drawn, created digitally, or taken from the internet (worth 60 points);
- The 12 Imperial symbols you chose and a brief description of the reason for the use and importance of each symbol (worth 150 points);
- The placement of each Imperial symbol shown and a brief description of the reason for its placement. Draw a line from the circle to the placement on the pao (worth 100 points); and
- Color should be considered regarding Bat Lóng Páo as well as for each of the symbols (worth 40 points).

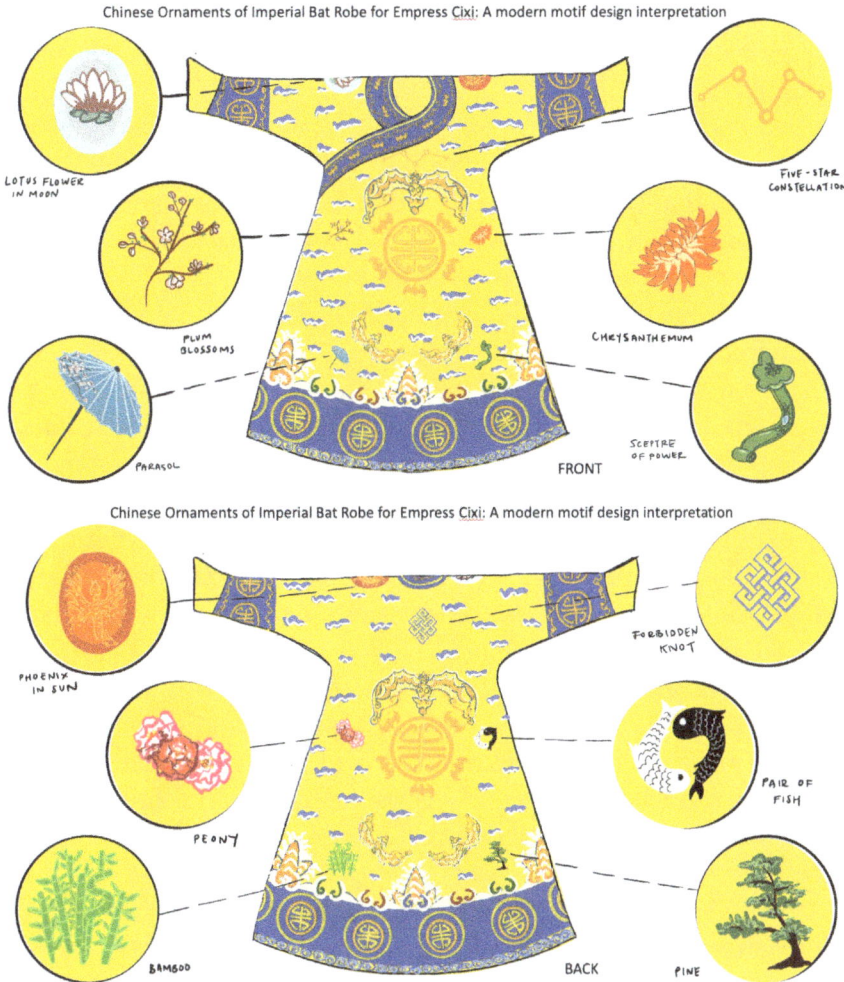

Figure 10.4 and Figure 10.5 Chinese ornaments of Imperial bat robe for Empress Cixi: A modern motif design interpretation: Front (Figure 10.4) and back (Figure 10.5)

Source: Madelyn Domagala, 2021

Every time I taught this course, I made significant changes, mostly because I tried to choose a new country to research and improve the quality of the content I was teaching. Before the pandemic, this usually meant grant writing and travel to a country to do in-person research on the ground, but the landscape of information available online from museums and collections exploded during the years of the pandemic as institutions moved their information online. I can confidently say traveling would be a luxury now, not a requirement. So much excellent information is available online, and there is incredible potential to have an expert join your class via Zoom.

What I also carefully evaluate each time I teach the course are the modules and arrangements of the countries. For the final project, I ask the students to consider the five "big ideas" or modules used during the course to connect topics in global fashion and adornment and how they have been shaped by history, religion, social class, gender identity and/or gender expression, ability/disability status, sexual orientation, and national origin. At this point in the semester, the student has greater insight into why I might have put a specific country in a specific module, with a better understanding that there are multiple, complex ideas at work and that clothing and dress are influenced by interconnected societies shaped by individuals of differing social class, gender, ethnicity, race, and group identities that intersect in complex and overlapping concepts.

In that final project, I ask each student to reassign ten countries/regions to different modules and submit their own examples and evidence of how race and ethnicity are shaped in the context of global fashion and costume and the interconnected nature of the diversity in culture and dress. (See Figure 10.2.) This serves as both an excellent exercise for the students and wonderful feedback about the course for me to better understand what the students have learned. I also ask that they create a new module topic they would like to see taught in the future to add to the list.

I am often asked, when faced with teaching the costume history of the entire globe, how I narrow down topics for lectures and projects. One piece of advice that has always served me well is to keep it relevant because you certainly cannot teach all the world's costume history in a single course. For example, we were studying India when the nation learned that Kamala Harris had been elected vice president, so I developed an assignment based around the Indian holiday of Diwali, the festival of lights, and what the costume and dress for newly elected Vice President Kamala Harris might be. What you can do is be sensitive to current international events and connect your assignments to topics your students are able to relate to.

11

The March of History Gives Way to Flowers in a Field

Chris Muller

School: New York University, Tisch School of the Arts

Course Title: Cultural History for the Designer

Major/General Education/Level: Required year-long course for all first-year costume, lighting, and set and production design graduate students

Usual Class Size: 18 students

Class Format: 3 hours weekly, in-person class

Texts or Materials Required: No required texts but a long list of suggested reading in many categories

Types of Access Needed: Students will use the internet, especially specific databases and collections; NYC-area libraries, museums, and collections; NYC-area sites.

Range of Material: As an overview of design and culture, the class is limited to everything ever created by all people throughout all of history.

Course Objectives
- The class deals with the contemporary issues of history and its meaning and uses, as well as the challenge of deep research in the age of effortless googling;
- In rejecting a linear approach to history as inherently Eurocentric and colonial, we try, as a group, to create a new form in which our understanding of things and events can be placed;

- ◆ We try to de-center the teacher as the sole repository of expertise, letting the instructor be part of the group who shares insights (with a margin of respect for being older);
- ◆ The offer is made to each student to give a presentation at some scheduled point on some topic of special interest that the rest of the class would benefit from, possibly informed by their cultural traditions or entirely personal interests or fascinations. Subject matter and form of presentation are entirely up to the student, with no need to 'clear' it with the instructor. Possible forms and character of a presentation are modeled by the instructor, but the student has complete agency over their 15-to-25-minute presentation.
- ◆ The structure to emerge over the course of two semesters is the beginning of a web of connections that will continue to grow through a lifetime of designing and living – any *thing* is related to economics, materials, social structures, gender, power structures, day-to-day experience, extraordinary events, etc.

Upon my accepting the assignment to teach the class on the history of clothing and architecture, the previous, longtime instructor handed me the syllabus, which had been written in 1969 and had been augmented and tweaked but otherwise still served as the foundation of the course – the logic being that the successive generations of students who took the course would have a shared vocabulary of design history.

Of course, the class was resolutely Eurocentric, though discussion of other cultures had been given moments in the narrative, with Africa, the Indian subcontinent, China, the Americas, and others appearing at the historic moments of European encounters.

We quickly decided to leave this model behind without a clear idea of what to do instead and have spent the last few years exploring new pedagogies, essentially experimenting on our students. It took some time to really grasp the meaning of what we were rejecting. The first impulse was to acknowledge the inadequacy of a timeline that focused almost entirely on Anglo-European design and history and create a timeline that included all histories, moving through time to look at as many cultures as possible. But even beyond being such a large undertaking that it would render the class more general in its lessons rather than less so, it soon became clear that the very idea of a linear historical approach – the march of history, from prehistoric man straight down to us – is a false construction meant to support a white supremacist view of culture.

Since the Renaissance and its re-enchantment with the ancient (Greek and Roman) world, history as a subject has been used by Europeans to link themselves to the glories of the past and suggest that they are carrying these traditions forward. With the belief that the best achievements of selectively chosen past cultures have been handed down to the present dominant culture, an excuse is at hand to dominate anyone outside that chain of cultures. The popular pageants of the Renaissance, where great figures would move in a procession past the duke or king or emperor, bestowing their approval and praise and permission to dominate, is the hidden model behind something even as simple as the march of clothes and armor in a book like Racinet's *Le Costume Historique*.

At first, rather than trying to encompass millennia of design history in a semester or two, like the feeling of a stone skipping over deeper waters, we tried the experiment of spending an entire semester looking at a single day in history. Like James Joyce's *Ulysses*, we pursued many different angles and points of view for our day, looking at sources to discover the literature on sale in bookstores, the music being played, the buildings being constructed, the wars being fought, the clothes being worn. It was interesting because we could choose literally any day that ever occurred – in the end, we looked at October 24, 1929, the day of the stock market crash; June 25, 1906, the day Stanford White was murdered; April 30, 1939, the opening day of the 1939 World's Fair; and June 28, 1969, the first day of the Stonewall uprising.

For NYU students, these events were all local, having left traces in the New York City they each experienced daily. Each class would look at some issue of culture, race, gender, fashion, socio-economics, etc., with the students each researching and reporting on an individual alive on the day under inspection. When possible, experts on certain topics were brought in as guests; they tapped the NYU pool of faculty and research. They sought out primary sources like newspaper archives and other media prominent from the time.

The semester ended with the students divided into groups, devising and performing some theatrical moment inspired by a theme, event, or person they had discovered along the way.

This was fascinating, certainly, and hopefully planted in the students the idea that any moment in history is similarly rich and deep, with many aspects and points of view to consider. It was interesting, though, that by the end of each semester, I still had the feeling that so much had been left unexplored and discussed – 14 weeks spent on a single day still left more unsaid than said.

We have moved on to another format for the class, now using a thematic approach tied to materials and theatre practice. These topics were chosen for their resonance with as many cultures and time periods as possible and deliberately bounce around week to week.

A given topic is usually preceded by a selection of short readings sent out the week before, along with a homework assignment that encourages creative thinking tied to the topic.

An example topic: The History of Blue. The ensuing discussion would include the following related content: Lapis lazuli, indigo, the physics of blue, blue-and-white china, the blues, and new blues.

For this class, the students will have read selections from *Color: A Natural History of the Palette* by Victoria Finlay, *Blue: The History of the Color* by Michel Pastoreau, and a few poems from different cultures that reference or meditate on the color blue. Students will also have a link to a podcast from NPR's Radiolab about color and perception. They could listen to a Spotify playlist of blue-themed music, including the blues. For their homework, they were invited to paint or draw a blue object or a study in blue, perhaps while listening to the podcast or the playlist.

The class itself explores the global story of the color and how it was created as a pigment. We investigate its changing symbolic meaning, looking at painting, ceramics, textiles, building materials, and lights. We look at the lapis mines in Afghanistan and the process and economics of indigo as a textile dye, the spread of Chinese blue-and-white china, and the use of laundry bluing as a pigment in African sculpture. We look at artists and art forms that deliberately simplify their palette or means of expression, like Picasso's blue period or the tradition of American blues. The final media shown is a segment from Derek Jarman's film *Blue*, which consists of just a blue field on the screen while Jarman and other performers speak a text about mortality. The students share their blue-themed homework and end the class on a celebratory note.

Also, an important part of each class is the student's personal presentations, referred to earlier, in which, generally, two students each week give a

---

Other topics we have explored so far in the class include:

Race and Entertainment in the United States;

A History of the World in Six Textiles;

A History of the World in Six Lights;

A History of the World in Six Building Materials; and

Cultures of Death and Mourning

Previous semester-long topics like the Stonewall uprising have made a reappearance as weekly topics.

Table 11.1 Syllabus Calendar

Week	Topic	Reading	Homework

1	Introduction
	The History of History of This
	The Procession of (Eurocentric) Time and an Audience of One
	The Path versus the Field
	The Uses of History
	Goals of the class:
	  How to research
	  Research binder as a design tool
	  Drawing your research
		Excerpt from *Braiding Sweetgrass: Indigenous Wisdom Scientific Knowledge,'* by Robin Will Kimmerer
		Excerpt from *1491: New Revelations of the Americas Before Columbus*, by Charles Mann
			Draw a Native American object – give source and provenance

2	The Land We Occupy The Leni Lenape and Manhattan A Journey Along Broadway, 1400 CE The North American Continent, 1491 The Mound Civilizations A Journey Along the Mississippi, 1400 CE Mass Pandemic and the Mini Ice Age Case Studies: Lenni Lenape Structures and Enclosures Washoe Aesthetics	'No "Thing to Wear": A Brief History of Kimono and Inappropriation from Japonisme to Kimono Protests,' by Michelle Liu Carriger	

(*Continued*)

Table 11.1 Continued

Week	Topic	Reading	Homework
3	Meet at the Met Museum Museums and Appropriation The Uses of History Reception Studies Art versus Artifact History of Display Voice of Authority Culture, Appropriation, and Trophies of Dominance Case Study: West African Sculpture in European and American Museums Embodied History, Trailing History – Monuments and Change Celebration, Subjugation, Invisibility Case Study: The Washington Monument Case Study: Statue of Teddy Roosevelt and the American Museum of Natural History	Readings: *Color: A Natural History of the Palette*, by Victoria Finlay; *Blue: The History of the Color*, by Michel Pastoreau Homework: A blue painting	
4	The History of Blue Lapis Lazuli Indigo The Physics of Blue Blue-and-White China The Blues New Blues	Excerpts from *The Little Devil in America*. by Hanif Abdurraqib; *Whose Blues? Facing Up to Race and the Future of Music*, by Adam Gussow	

The March of History Gives Way to Flowers in a Field ◆ 179

5	Race and Entertainment Black Culture and the Birth of American Music (and Theatre and Film and Radio and Television and Animation and . . .) Minstrelsy and Black Face Case Study: Bert Williams, 'The Funniest Man I Ever Saw, the Saddest Man I Ever Knew' Case Study: 5 into 8: Pentatonic African Scale and the Western Octave Celebration of Black Excellence	Excerpt from *Fragments for a History of the Human Body*, edited by Michel Feher Homework: Draw a human body	
6	The History of the Body Body Theory Silhouette as a History of Sexiness West Africa Ancient Egypt 1950s United States The Djenne and the Limitless Body Body Modification	Excerpt, *Women's Work*, by Elizabeth Wayland Barber	Drawing of fabric texture
7	History of the World in Six Textiles String, Linen, Silk, Cotton, Wool, Rayon Case Study: West African Textiles, a Research Project with Ari Fulton	Excerpts from *The Morbid Anatomy Anthology*, edited by Joanna Ebenstein	Day of the Dead drawing

(*Continued*)

Table 11.1 Continued

Week	Topic	Reading	Homework
8	Cultures of Death and Mourning Mourning Miniatures Mummification and Afterlives Hamlet, Purgatory, and Ghosts Mortifications Memento Mori	Excerpt from *Disenchanted Night: The Industrialization of Light in the Nineteenth Century*, by Wolfgang Shivelbusch	Draw a lamp or other light source
9	Class meets at 6 p.m. History of the World in Six Lights The Sun, Fire, Oil Lamp, Limelight, Incandescent, LEDs Walking at Night – Leni Schwendinger, guest		Write a two-page paper about light and walking Draw materials study of one: Timber, stone, brick, concrete, steel, glass
10	History of the World in Six Building Materials Timber, Stone, Brick, Concrete, Steel, Glass Case Study: The Pantheon, a Secret Rediscovered Case Study: Contemporary Nigerian Architecture, Renua Isueli, guest	Excerpt from *Flash of the Spirit* by Robert Farris Thompson	Study of African American (Pan-American) artwork
11	Diaspora and Syncretism When Cultures Collide: Forced Belief and Absorption Diaspora Americas: New York City, the African City, C. Daniel Dawson, guest Orisa on Ayé – African Deities in the Americas		Draw a queer hero

12	Stonewall: Before and After Queer in America Before the Uprising A Brick in a Purse in a Car Window – The Uprising A Gay Overview of All Times, Everywhere Gay Bar Culture in New York – A History, Qweenjean, guest

Source: Chris Muller

15-minute presentation on a topic of personal interest they feel would be of benefit for us to all learn. This assignment, given with minimal guidelines, has been very successful. Examples have included a familial history of corn pone bread, a guide to different African American traditions in the South, and the meaning of different recipes – a presentation given while the student made corn pone using their family's recipe, to be then shared with the class; another presentation was a history of hair coloring and dying, given by a student who themselves sported a different hair color weekly, which was extremely well researched and a topic about which I knew very little.

Since this is a two-semester class, I've enlisted the students in helping shape the second semester. After the fall semester, they see what the class is doing, so at semester's end, I elicit their ideas for topics to cover in the spring. We craft the spring syllabus together with topics the students are interested in, many having to do with identity politics, as well as sequels to classes in the first semester. For instance, the class A History of the World in Six Textiles is continued with Contemporary Textiles and the Future of Textiles. The burden of research is moved from my shoulders entirely to be shared by the students – one of the key elements of de-centering the 'expert' teacher.

Reflections

The major impetus in the class moves away from a fixed, seemingly unchanging body of knowledge the students are meant to memorize towards a shifting, never-the-same-from-year-to-year experience. To be sure, there are students who would much prefer a set series of facts they could master, but for others, this is a more active, participatory exercise. For me, it changes the workload – not necessarily increasing or decreasing but shifting its emphasis, and each year is a new adventure.

12
Activities for the Classroom

Project A: Worn History
Personal History Through Clothes

Debra Krajec

School: Marquette University

Department, Area, or School Within the School: Theatre Arts Program, Department of Digital Media and Performing Arts

Course Title: THAR 4230: History of Clothing II: From Jane Austen through Austin Powers

Major/General Education/Level: This is an undergraduate class, offered as part of the university core curriculum in the Expanding Our Horizons Discovery Tier. With this recent change in status, the audience for the class audience has changed from theatre majors to all majors.

Project Size: Individual

Project Format: Could be in person or online; final product could be a paper, a presentation, or a video.

Texts, Materials, or Access Required for This Project: None

Project Learning Outcomes

In addition to recognizing the historical period to which these garments belong, the student should be able to:

EXAMINE dress as a means of personal expression in each historical period;
RECOGNIZE non-verbal messages sent through the wearing of clothes;

EMPATHIZE with those from different social strata who wore these clothes; and
DISCUSS fashion as social history.

Submission Format
Usually submitted as a written essay with photos at the end of the semester. Could be a public presentation to class or a video creation.

I needed a project that would require my students, especially my STEM students, many of whom struggle with visual research and recognition of silhouette and detail changes, to find a personal connection to fashion history. As my history of clothing courses are now open to the entire undergraduate population, it has required me to rethink the way I teach them. I am not teaching students who are used to visual research or even historical research of "things" instead of events, and I realized I needed to break away from the traditional assignments and lectures I have always given. These students need more examples, more explanations, and a reason why this study matters. These are rarely students who study history. I have tried several new projects and approaches in my classes to make the material relevant and interesting, and I know I have a long way to go. This small project was created to change the pace of the course for a wider range of students.

I wanted students to realize that garments have meaning and can serve as markers of human life stories. This project gives them the opportunity to find ways that a piece of clothing has been an important part of a person's history in a tangible way and to reflect on how clothing is part of all our lives. While this project deals with only one garment, it enables the student to find out more than what it looks like, what it was made of, or how it was made; they discover what the garment has meant to the wearer and how it became part of their history.

This project is quite different from other assignments in the course as it rarely concerns high fashion or famous people. It brings to the forefront the concept that clothing is an item that allies us as humans. The stories are as important as the garments. The personal memory is why the garment has meaning.

Many students have really enjoyed this project as it doesn't require them to stay in the unfamiliar world of high fashion and style trends. Of course, they have to determine how the chosen garment fits within the historical period and how it might be different from the mainstream due to the economic, religious, gender, or social status of the wearer. But it is a personal connection, an important event, a touching memory about which they are learning. My impression is that personal stories are a good way to model my basic goal for the class, as stated in my syllabus:

We will be studying fashion – what people wore and what influenced these styles. Everyone wears clothing of some variety in our Western culture. It is a part of who we are, how we relate to our world, and how we feel about ourselves. Consider this class to be an observatory of sorts . . .

Assignment Guidelines

WORN HISTORY – Personal History Through Clothes

Some articles of clothing have special meaning to us. That sweater that was your dad's favorite, the prom dress that looked chic on your grandma in high school, the old Little League baseball uniform your uncle wore the first time he hit a home run, the old army jacket from Vietnam, Grandpa's tie from his wedding day in Puerto Rico, Great Aunt Sally's purse she bought in Paris before the war . . .

Clothes hold memories and meaning. They can remind us of happy times or tough times. Most people have a piece of clothing they have kept, even though it may not fit and might be decades out of style or old and shabby, that reminds them of someone, of some time, of some special or difficult event.

I would like you to write a short essay (or create a public presentation or a video to share with the class) on such a garment – it can be a relative's or a dear friend's – and tell the story behind the garment, explain the meaning this garment has for the owner. This will require you to interview the person and find out answers to the following questions:

> What did this garment mean to you at the point in time that you wore it?
> What does it mean to you now?
> How did you acquire it?
> Why has it been kept?
> Has the garment changed through time?
> Have others worn it?

You will also need to be able to discuss how the garment reflects the fashion of the period to which it belongs. Then, reflect on what you learned from doing this project – both about fashion history and about the meaning of clothes. What is different about researching an actual garment and who wore it, instead of researching a style of garment from history?

The garment should be over 20 years old. It does not have to be American or "Western." I recommend that this garment have originated with someone at least one generation older than yourself; older might be even more interesting. If you do not have someone close to you who has such a garment, please make inquiries in your community and find someone with a memorable garment. This may be a chance for you to make a connection with a new friend through your interest in their "worn history." If you can, include photos.

Student Example from Vanessa Lattas, 2022

On an ordinary day during the height of World War II, my pre-teen grandfather managed to save enough money to buy himself his first fisherman's cap in a small Greek town called Alykes on the island of Zakynthos. Owning and smugly sporting the hat meant that my grandfather was finally graduating from being a boy to becoming a man, from having petty farm responsibilities to having exciting fishing obligations, and from tolerating monotony and isolation in the mountains to enjoying the thrill and liberation promised by the Ionian Sea (with necessary protection from the sun also offered by the garment). Most, if not all, of the small-town population of men were either sailors, fishermen, or aiding the war effort by training for and/or enlisting in the Greek navy. And so, one could imagine how desperately every young Greek boy at the time dreamt of becoming a fisherman or sailor like their fathers when they grew up. It follows that choosing, being sized for, acquiring, and wearing their own fisherman's cap was symbolic of a dream beginning to come true.

The fisherman's caps that my family has preserved and archived are actually not the first ones my grandfather got, but rather the last ones he bought before he immigrated to the US (Figure 12.1). They were made and bought in Tripoli, Greece, where my grandfather visited his extended family to say his

Figure 12.1 Greek fisherman's cap

Source: Vanessa Lattas, 2022

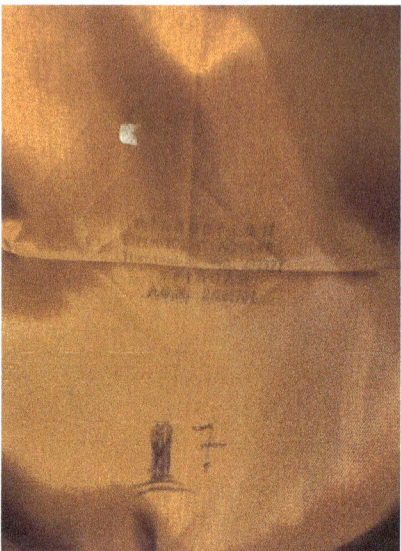

Figure 12.2 Interior of Greek fisherman's cap. The size 8 of the hat is crossed out and re-drawn as a 7.

Source: Vanessa Lattas, 2022

last goodbyes before boarding a boat to the States. My grandfather loved to constantly re-tell this humorous story about being sized for one of the hats. The story goes that the vendor he went to insisted that his head measurements were consistent with a hat size of 8, but my grandfather worried that if he were to Greek dance with the hat on (Greek island dancing frequently involves bending down to touch the feet and floor), it could fall if it was just the right size for him and inevitably stretched out as it was used. Therefore, my grandfather pleaded that the man sell him a size 7. The man explained over and over again why it would not be a smart choice to size down, and he even underlined the "8" he wrote on the inside of the hat (Figure 12.2) as he offered his advice. But my grandfather, being the stubborn, "I am never wrong" man he was, convinced the man to sell him a size 7. Fortunately, it ended up being a great choice because the slightly shorter visor on the cap is what helped my grandma see how handsome my grandpa was without him needing to look up, and so she could crush on him at the restaurant she worked at inconspicuously while he read the menu and newspaper. The size 7 hats also now fit my uncles' heads perfectly! Moreover, the cap also allowed my grandpa to meet his first friend in the US: A fellow Greek immigrant named Andreas who also couldn't speak English fluently but knew he could befriend someone who was guaranteed to speak Greek since that someone was wearing the beloved, easily identifiable Greek fisherman's cap. They ended up being best friends for over 40 years until my grandfather's final days (Figure 12.3).

Activities for the Classroom ◆ 189

Figure 12.3 Interior band of a Greek fisherman's cap, noting that it is made in Greece

Source: Vanessa Lattas, 2022.

Figure 12.4 Greek flag, drawing of a Greek fisherman's boat, and fisherman's caps

Source: Vanessa Lattas, 2022

Overall, the fisherman caps that my family has from my grandfather are not only reminders of his presence now that he is physically gone but also symbolic of pride for Greek culture and hallmarks of my familial immigrant experience (Figure 12.4). I am constantly in awe of the fact that they are of such high-quality wool and in such good condition, and I cannot wait until my little brother is old enough to flaunt them. My greatest hope is that they continuously get passed down to be admired and cherished for generations to come.

Project B: Final Assignment
World Building

Brenda Van der Wiel

School: The University of Utah

Department, Area, or School Within the School: Department of Theatre

Course Title: History of Costume and Material Culture

Major/General Education/Level: Upper-level undergraduate class

Project Size: Individual

Project Format: In person or online; final product could be a paper, a presentation, or a video

Texts, Materials, or Access Required for this Project: Online learning platform

---

Course Description

History of Costume and Material Culture is a required class for all students in the Performing Arts Design program at the University of Utah. Through visually supported lectures and research projects, students are immersed in the history of clothing and material culture throughout the world. The social and historical influences that affect history are examined. Research methods are explored and practiced. Finally, students will use gathered research facts in a creative world-building project that mirrors the research work that should go into the production design process. Currently, this is an upper-level course, but students have suggested that they would have benefitted from the research methodology information much earlier in their educational track.

Project Learning Outcomes

- Conduct research about a range of time periods, geographic locations, and cultures;
- Apply the history of clothing and material culture knowledge to design choices and make personal judgements about the validity of those choices; and
- Gain competency and confidence in justifying design choices in both a written and verbal format.

After several years of attempting to add a non–Western European curriculum to an already-full one-semester class that was to cover all costume and material culture history, I realized this was an unreasonable and unsatisfying task for both instructor and student. Being part of a summer collective of like-minded professors working to end the strict adherence to "teaching the timeline" led me to this new course format. Focusing the class on deeper dives into fewer subjects while providing good research methodology skills seemed like a more effective way to structure the class. I wanted to add a creative final project that would incorporate the student's research findings into valid artistic choices. In talking to a group of students one day about their weekend plans, several were competing in a virtual game–playing event. As they talked, this final project idea was formed.

Fall of 2021 was the first time this revised course was taught, and student response to the class was overwhelmingly positive. One student commented that all the classwork, but especially the final project was "engaging and relatable to real life scenarios." Based on the high quality of the work completed for this final project, I would agree that students were engaged and invested in the learning.

Assignment Guidelines

Character 1* is unhappy with some aspect of their current life. Describe why your character and their entourage are dissatisfied with some aspect of life and what they are escaping from.

* From a Western European culture from 15th–18th century

Character 2** is unhappy with some aspect of their current life. Describe why your character and their entourage are dissatisfied with some aspect of life and what they are escaping from.
** From a non–Western European culture earlier than the 15th century

They both search for a deserted island in order to create their own utopia.
But they both arrive at the same island.
All they have is their frame of reference with which to try and create a new way of living.
But they are committed to not having one culture colonize another. They hope to blend the two into a new culture, maybe taking the best of each or maybe creating something entirely new and different.
What is your world's governing system?
What social difference exists between people?
If the character is trying to escape from something, how have those things shaped this new world?
What technologies from each character's former life have been incorporated into this new world?
Write three to four pages, comprehensively describing the previous lives of Character 1 and Character 2, as well as exploring the answers to the questions on the previous slide and any other creative information you have decided on. This can be written in a creative manner like a novel or movie pitch.
What are those activities in this new world, and where do they happen? What are they doing? (Three set sketches.)
Design clothing for each of the places settings you have described: Maybe a dressed-up night out (the most elite), a laborer, another costume for a specific experience that happens in your world. (Three costume sketches.)
Music to accompany each of your settings or each of your costumes. Explain the history of the music and why you chose the individual pieces of music. (Three music mash-ups, one for each activity or place setting.) Free mp3 downloads, Podcastle.ai is a free online tool where you can mix tracks (uses Chrome).
What is the quality of the lighting?
Is there electricity or candles or torches?
What does that mean for the way people live?
Include at least four images of the quality of light for each of three events.
You can bring one modern piece of technology (video and media design) into this world. What is it, and how is it incorporated into the new world? (One explanation of modern technology.)

Figure B.1 Final project room sketch for World Building: Project incorporating the worlds of Anne Hathaway and Empress Wu Zetian

Source: Sam Dalton, 2022

Final Project: Partial Written Work for World Building Project Incorporating the Worlds of Anne Hathaway and Empress Wu Zetian

Student: Sam Dalton

Technology

During the Tang dynasty, a wide variety of technological growth happened; when Empress Wu left her nation, she brought much of it with her, including timekeeping, advanced structural engineering, fireworks, and a new art: Woodblock printing. Anne brought with her some historical texts of other societies, as well as medicines; her love of books dragged her to bring along a printing press and a variety of the newest tools and machines created to make life a bit easier for the Renaissance artists. Each had very efficient sailing ships and a strong ability to map and navigate, but the Empress brought with her a greater understanding of how to utilize the materials around her, whereas the English weren't familiar with creating from scratch.

As these two societies merged their technological systems, it was settled that they should embrace the strengths that each had to offer and not let their

Figure B.2 Final project costume sketch for World Building project incorporating the worlds of Anne Hathaway and Empress Wu Zetian

Source: Sam Dalton, 2022

egos get in the way. The Tang engineering was far superior to anything the English had handy, so they took over construction, and most of their architecture was more heavily Chinese but incorporated strong homages to the English to help them feel more welcome. The English had the responsibility of taking over record-keeping for the new nation, their printing press made it easier to create historical documents, and faster than copying everything by hand.

Modern Technology

I have decided that their modern technology will be a light rail system. Effective public transportation is the key to successfully growing any community; this will not only help them build stronger ties as they unite but also make it easier as they build their new community.

Final World Building Project; 16 points Possible Rubric

	2	1.5	1	.5	Points Earned
Content: Written facts on the characters and the world	Google Slide presentation is an especially clear presentation of the topic. An abundance of facts and details are presented.	Google Slide presentation provides a clear presentation of the topic. Many facts and details are presented.	Google Slide presentation provides some information about the topic, but some details and/or facts may be missing.	Google Slide presentation is missing a lot of required information.	
Content: Spaces	The designs are based on the research presented. The design shows a clear understanding of the research in its use.	The designs are based somewhat on the research presented. The design shows an understanding of the research in its use, but some things may be made up or not supported by research.	The designs are not always based on the research presented. The design lacks some understanding of the research in its use.	The designs are not based on the research presented, or the research is not present. The design lacks understanding of the research in its use.	

Content: Costumes	The designs are based on the research presented. The design shows a clear understanding of the research in its use.	The designs are based somewhat on the research presented. The design shows an understanding of the research in its use, but some things may be made up or not supported by research.	The designs are not always based on the research presented. The design lacks some understanding of the research in its use.	The designs are not based on the research presented, or the research is not present. The design lacks understanding of the research in its use.
Content: Lighting	The designs are based on the research presented. The design shows a clear understanding of the research in its use.	The designs are based somewhat on the research presented. The design shows an understanding of the research in its use, but some things may be made up or not supported by research.	The designs are not always based on the research presented. The design lacks some understanding of the research in its use.	The designs are not based on the research presented, or the research is not present. The design lacks understanding of the research in its use.

(*Continued*)

Continued

	2	1.5	1	.5	Points Earned
Content: Music	The designs are based on the research presented. The design shows a clear understanding of the research in its use.	The designs are based somewhat on the research presented. The design shows an understanding of the research in its use, but some things may be made up or not supported by research.	The designs are not always based on the research presented. The design lacks some understanding of the research in its use.	The designs are not based on the research presented, or the research is not present. The design lacks understanding of the research in its use.	
Design	Each slide is laid out with good design thought. The images add to the information given.	Each slide is laid out with acceptable design thought. The images generally add to the information given.	The slides do use images, but some of the images may not go along with the information, or the number of images is not what was asked for.	Not enough images are included in the presentation, or they are laid out poorly.	

	Used four or more sources. Sources need to be included in presentation.	Used three sources. Sources need to be included in presentation.	Used two sources. Sources need to be included in presentation.	Used only one source. Sources need to be included in presentation.
Sources				
Presentation	The presentation engaged the audience. The delivery showed the student was comfortable with understanding and incorporating the research into their design.	The presentation mostly engaged the audience. The delivery showed the student was fairly comfortable with understanding and incorporating the research into their design. There may have been a few stumbles and having to relook up information.	The presentation did not always engage the audience. The delivery showed the student was somewhat uncomfortable with understanding and incorporating the research into their design.	The presentation did not engage the audience. The delivery showed the student was quite uncomfortable with understanding and incorporating the research into their design.

Project C: Historic Tools and Techniques

An Exercise in Material Culture Observation

Ashley Bellet

School: Purdue University

Department: Department of Theatre, School of Design, Art, and Performance

Course Title: Period Style for the Theatre

Major/General Education/Level: Open to all students, primarily taken by theatre graduate and undergraduate students

Project Size: Individual

Project Format: In-person discussion

Texts, Materials, or Access Required for this Project: None on the part of the students

---

Project Learning Objectives

To examine an unfamiliar object in detail;
To imagine the object in use based on observations of the object itself;
To experience an object separate from immediate context; and
If possible, to apply these skills in an archive.

Assignment Outline

Materials Needed
A variety of tools that may be unfamiliar or uncommon; tools that are specific to a process, a craft, or a technique. They may be modern or antique – they simply need to serve a function. (See Figure C.1 for examples.)

Process
Outline the following directions *before* distributing the objects.

No phones or internet are allowed.

Before you say anything out loud, look closely at your object. Take notes on the color, size, shape, and any details you see:

What does it look like? Is it familiar?
What does it feel like? Is it heavy?
Is it comfortable in the hand? Is it large or small?
Does it smell or make any sounds?
Is it old? Is it new? How do you know? and

Take the time to draw the object. As Susan Crabtree famously said, "Drawing is seeing."

Distribute the tools to individuals or groups of two or three people.

Allow students 15 to 20 minutes to experience the objects and document their notes following the questions listed earlier.

After making these notes, ask the students to imagine what the tool is for and perhaps what it may be called.

Moving around the room, ask the students to describe three to five reasons they came to the conclusions they did. Were there details that seemed important, or others that seemed less important? If the students are in groups, was there a disagreement as to the function of the object?

Reflection Questions

What initial assumptions did you make about the object you received? What were these assumptions based on? Size? Wear? Your own experiences? The source of the object?

Did you look around at the other objects in the room and seek to compare or contextualize them?

Were you surprised to discover the primary use of the object? Why or why not?
How does it feel to encounter an object that you have never seen before? Were you able to tell its importance? Was it used daily or on occasion? Who would use a tool like this? How do you think it affected their work, their bodies, and their station? Do you think this is an expensive object? How might this relate to finding objects in an archive?

Taking the Next Step When Possible

In the subsequent class period, take the students to investigate an archive you have nearby. It may be located in a department, in the library, or in a local museum. Using the questions posed earlier, ask the students to reflect on an object they find.

Following this archive trip, have students research the object to learn more and practice contextualizing it.

Alternative Approaches

A Tool With Two Stories

Many artisans transfer tools from one part of their lives to another part for use in new and helpful ways. One way to approach this project might be to gather some of these multi-use tools and have students start with their primary use, then work together to understand a possible second or third use – specifically for hand crafts.

Example: A basic toothbrush. While most of us recognize the primary use of a basic toothbrush, many artisans use them as spattering tools, cleaning tools, brushes for suede, or brushes to remove chalk lines from clothing. When we find alternate uses for familiar tools, what does that say about where and how we work? What does it say about other tools that may or may not be available? Imagine a story of how one tool came to be used for a new purpose.

A Tool of the Past

This option works well if the students are very familiar with the tool(s).

Imagine that the year is 3035. You have come across an object you have never seen before, and this is it. Observe the object closely and imagine what it might have been used for, based solely on the details of the object itself.

If the tool is related to sewing, imagine a world where all clothes are made by machine. How else might someone – with no connection to or awareness of a sewing machine – interpret this tool? If the tool is from a kitchen or home, imagine a world where cooking, cleaning, and general chores are outsourced or unnecessary, thus no longer familiar to most people.

Now take a moment to acknowledge that people of the past engaged with things in a very different way. There are crafts, daily activities, and events that we no longer take part in. What can objects tell us, and how does our own contemporary lens affect our view of objects from the past?

Things to Consider

Many students' first instinct was to go straight to Google before I had finished offering instructions. Be sure to be very clear about these boundaries beforehand.

For those students involved in the costume shop, I had to be very picky about which tools to give them. Many had at least briefly encountered most of the tools, so I had to move beyond my own crafting tool kit for new objects. I pulled from all theatre shops, my kitchen, and my garage. Their

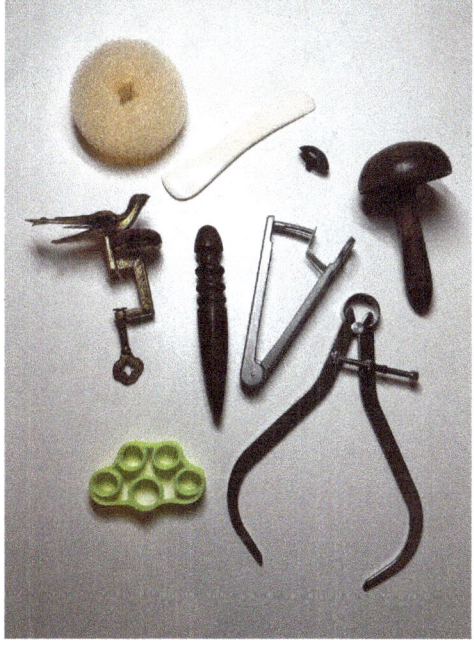

Figure C.1 A few of the tools I like to use for this activity

knowledge of my own work and hobbies helped them figure out several of the tools – which is great contextualization though it succeeds from a different perspective.

A wig rat, a bone tool, a bunion popper, a darning mushroom, a sewing bird, a leather burnishing tool, a cherry pitter, a finger strengthener, a caliper.

Conclusion

Ashley Bellet

Hopefully, in these pages, you have found inspiration and new resources: Books, articles, images, new projects, and new perspectives for discussion. Hopefully, you have also discovered a few new colleagues in this movement for change. We are all so eager to explore the work we are doing and want to support you in your work as well.

If there is anything we have discovered in assembling this resource, it is that there are innumerable ways to approach this course. You can change the format, the content, or simply the projects you give your students. You can engage outside resources or offer a variety of articles, leaving a core text behind. Alternatively, you can lean in to a new core text, digging into the resources it offers. You can combine the work of design with that of research or distinguish the two independently. There are endless options, and while the task itself may seem daunting, it can be – and will be – very exciting work.

Teaching this class is a project that must evolve, and the topics we find important today may not seem so important tomorrow. One quandary in higher education is the combination of legacy and exploration we look forward to in the classroom. Students may look forward to experiencing the stories they've heard about a certain class or professor, but it is a tricky thing to build an 'established' class. There is comfort in repeating content, just as there is security in repeating pedagogical methods; there is excitement in trying new methods and joy in trying new content. However, many desire the certainty in memorization and linear narratives, and while some desire to move away from those approaches, many of our students still learn this way.

Sometimes it is not about changing everything but changing some things, finding what fits – and continually re-examining those changes.

But remember, this is YOUR classroom.

We must face the reality that while one person's method may seem ideal, resonating with our own sense of history, in fact, that approach may not resonate with our students. Each of us encounters a different population, a different curricular challenge, and a different student zeitgeist each semester. Not every project will work in your classroom, and not every text will sit comfortably with your students.

Many of these instructors recommend moving away from playing the role of the expert in the classroom. This can be empowering for both you and your students, but it might also leave you with a sense of playing catch-up or feeling as if you need to improvise in making connections in the classroom. Improvisation is not for everyone, though we can make some beautiful discoveries when thinking and responding in the moment. When projects fall flat or lectures are met with silence, as teachers, we often turn this experience inward. We might consider one assignment a failure or one reading to be out of touch with our students. In fact, we have much to gain by flipping these challenges back into the classroom, asking our students to reflect on moments they appreciated and those they did not understand.

The reality is some of our efforts *will* fall flat. One semester, a project will be met with astounding success, and the following semester, it may feel rote or out of touch. The hours we spent prepping for class will feel pointless, and we will get frustrated. The best thing about teaching, however, is the same thing we love about theatre. We get to try again. There will be another semester, just as there will be another show. We will prepare ourselves with the knowledge and experience we've gained and be ready to take more chances again.

These chapters are not here to tell you what to do or how to do it but to take a moment, consider what motivates you, and to run with that in one of the many ways suggested. This may be an excellent moment to tear things to the ground or perhaps a better moment to nudge different projects into your syllabus. No matter which, it is time to take a chance and make a change. Our students are asking for change, and our universities desperately need it. This is a brilliant moment to be inspired by what is possible.

Index

Note: Page numbers in *italics* indicate figures, **bold** indicate tables in the text

15%, 4 Mood Board Projects, 17th–20th Century Fashion 40–41
15%, Group Research Project: Ancient World Dress 41

abridged clothing history 102–119; adaptability in 109; assessment 111; classes **118**; construction-based model in 107–109; course contents 111–119; course described 104–106; course objectives 104; critiques in 109–111; drawing and 109–111, *110*; learning outcomes 104; need for change in 107; shaping and slowing down during learning of 103–104; student responses 119; syllabus calendar **113–117**
active learning 3, 4
adaptability/adaptations: in abridged clothing history 109; people- and place-based curriculum 92–95
Adichie, C. 151
Adobe Sparks 28
African tunics *105*
Afrofuturism 59
American Theatrical Costume Association (ATCA) 1, 78, 167
Anderson, B. 107, 108
Anderson, C. 107, 108
Antionette, M. 17
artificial silhouette 107, 108
assessments: abridged clothing history 111; conscious fashion history **40**, 40–41; cultural connections 126–132
assignments: cultural connections 132–134; dress, history of 63–68; fashion and costume project 170–172; material culture project 201; personal history through clothes project 186; rubric for "read the label" 77; style 13; Western fashion history **146–150**, 151; world building project 192–193; worn history project 186

Bachelor of Arts (BA) 47, 81
Bat Lóng Páo 170
Baylor University 121
Benda, C. 59
Black Lives Matter 46, 68
Bloom's taxonomy 5
Blue (Jarman) 176
Blue: The History of the Color (Pastoreau) 176
Blum, S.D. 123
Boal, A. 122
body adornment *169*
Brewer, N. 137
Burnham, D. 56

CalArts Library 37–38, 42
California Institute of the Arts 34–35
Carrier, M. L. 57
Carter, R. E. 59
Catterall, S. 57
Center for Research on Learning and Teaching (CRLT) 167
cerulean monologue 151
Chapin, C. 1, 27, 78, 167
Checkerboard Tunic 30, 31
Chevalier D'Eon 39
Chun, M. K. 93
Cixi 170, *171*
clothing motifs 111–112

Color: A Natural History of the Palette (Finlay) 176
Connected Teaching (Schwartz) 78
conscious fashion history 34–44; basic vocabulary 40; catalyst for 37–40; course assessment **40**, 40–41; course objectives 36; course projects 40–41; expanded practice 35–37; learning outcomes 36; materials selection for reference and discussion 43; sample project 41–42; syllabus calendar **38–39**
contemporary dress *15*
conversational assessment 131–132; *see also* assessment
costume history *see* cultural connections; fashion and costume
Cottom, T. M. 57
course objectives: abridged clothing history 104; conscious fashion history 36; cultural connections 123; dress, history of 48–49; fashion and costume 160; issues of history 173–174; people- and place-based curriculum 84; research 25
COVID-19 24, 29, 68, 91, 158, 166
creative arts experience (CAE) 135
critical thinking 75, 142, 143
cultural connections 120–138; assessment 126–132; conversational assessment 131–132; course described 120–123; course objectives 123; curricular correlations 134–138; learning outcomes 124; research project assignment 132–134; semester goals 130; syllabus calendar **124–125**
cultural literacy 74
cura personalis 47
curriculum: committee 32; connections across 88–89; Magis Core 46, 67; people- and place-based 83–101; research 31–32
Cut My Cote (Burnham) 56, 60

The Danger of a Single Story (Adichie) 151
Deloria, P. 57
The Devil Wears Prada (film) 69, 151
Di Medici, C. 69
dress, history of 45–70; change 46–60; course objectives 48–49; Historic Garment Analysis Project Rubric **62**; kimono 60–61, *61*; learning outcomes 49–60; sample student assignment 63–68; syllabus calendar **50–54**
Dress Codes (Thompson) 56, 59
The Dress Detective 88, 94
Dressing the Resistance (Benda) 59
dyeing 56, 74, 80, 128, *129*

Edwards, L. 28
empathy 47, 75
Enlivening Cultural and Gender Identities Through Dress 142–143
environmental justice 128
ethnography-based case study 142, 151
expanded practice, conscious fashion history 35–37
experiential learning 84, 88, 92–93, 152–154

Fairfield University 47
fashion and costume 156–172; advice on 168; assignments 170–172; course creation phases 160, 166–169; course description 156–160; course objectives 160; learning outcomes 160; syllabus calendar **161–165**
Fashion and Costume: Global Adornment and Attire course 169
Fashion and Individual Expression (module) **52–54**, 58
Fashion and Socio-Economic Power (module) **50–51**
Fashion History: A Global View (Welters and Lillethun) 27, 40, 49, 71
female fashion 63, 66
field trips 68, 85, 90, 93, 128
Finlay, V. 176

fisherman: boat *189*; caps *187–189*, 187–190
Fishman, B. 167
flipped classroom 4
Free People kimono 61
Freire, P. 122
Fujiwara Court dress *110*

gameful learning pedagogy 167
general education *see* undergraduate general education
The Golden Thread (St. Clair) 28

hands-on exercises 105
Harris, K. 172
Hathaway, A. 151
Herrera, J. *106*
Historic Garment Analysis Project Rubric **62**
historic tools and techniques *see* material culture (project)
history, issues of course 173–182; objectives 173–174; reflections on 182; syllabus calendar **177–181**
History of Costume (Payne) 42
How to Read a Dress and *How to Read a Suit* (Edwards) 28

Industrial Revolution 18, 19
interviews, people- and place-based curriculum 90
"The Invention of the Suit" 48

Jarman, D. 176
Jirousek, C. 57

Kānaka Maoli 93
Kent State University 23–24, 27
kimono 60–61, *61*
Kimumu 94
Kotowska, N. 63–68, *64*

Lauhala, K. 93
Lauhala weaving 98–99, *98–99*

Leading Change: Go Beyond Gamification with Gameful Learning 167
learning objectives: material culture project 200; undergraduate general education 74
learning outcomes: abridged clothing history 104; conscious fashion history 36; cultural connections 124; fashion and costume 160; people- and place-based curriculum 84–88; research 26; undergraduate general education 74–75; Western fashion history 144; world building project 191; worn history project 184–185
Le Costume Historique (Racinet) 175
Lieber, C. 59
Lillethun, A. 27, 40, 49, 71
linear narrative 93, 95, 205
Liz Lerman's Critical Response Process 111
Los Angeles County High School of the Arts (LACHSA) 102–103, 107

Magis Core curriculum 46; *see also* curriculum
male fashion 63, 66
Marcinkiewicz, J. 27–28
Marquette University 184
massive open online course (MOOC) 167
material culture project 200–204; archive trip for students 202; assignment 201; learning objectives 200; multi-use tools 202; Purdue University 200; reflection questions 201–202; tool(s) 202–203, *203*
Mayer, Adti 59
McConnell, K. 59
meaningful, defined 36
Mentges, G. 59
Middle East and North Africa (MENA) 127
Minoan: standing loom *136*; weaving 135
Miso 153
modules **8–10**; dress, history of **50–54**; global adornment and attire **161–165**;

hands-on activity 98–99, *98–99*; mind map of *159*; people- and place-based curriculum **85**
Montclair State University 7–8, 11
Muller, C. 69
multi-use tools 202
Myers, C. 1, 27, 167

Niemer, R. 167
Nilsen, K. 93

object-based approach *see* style
Orientalism (Said) 57
Ottoman Dress and Design in the West (Jirousek and Catterall) 57

parade of fashion approach 157–158, 167
passive learning 4, 33
Pastoreau, M. 176
Payne, B. 42
pedagogical approach 3, 4, 33
The Pedagogy of the Oppressed (Freire) 122
people- and place-based curriculum 83–101; adaptations 92–95; connections across 88–89; construction module hands-on activity 98–99, *98–99*; course objectives 84; course redesign process 90–92; cumulative class portfolio/journal 89; discussion and lecture on fibers, dyestuffs 95–98, *96–97*; discussion in class 89; field trip experiences 90; interviews 90; learning outcomes 84–88; modules **85**; object analysis project 90; shared vocabulary 88; syllabus calendar **85–88**; weekly collaborative journal prompts 99–101, *100*; *see also* curriculum
personal history through clothes (project): assignment 186; learning outcomes 184–185; personal history through clothes 186–187; submission format 185–186; Vanessa Lattas, 2022 *187–189*, 187–190

Playing Indian (Deloria) 57
presentation rubric (weekly homework) **30**
Priestly, M. 69, 151
Putra, A. 127

race and ethnicity (R/E) 168–169
Racinet, A. 175
ReDressing the Narrative costume history pedagogy workshop 167
re-fashioning time 18–21
research, fashion history and technology 23–33; Checkerboard Tunic *30*, 31; course description 23; course objectives 25; curriculum 31–32; learning outcomes 26; perspective 25–31; presentation rubric (weekly homework) **30**; slow and fast changes 24; students' projects 29; style 12–15, 19–20; syllabus calendar **26–27**
research methodology 74
Roots of Fashion (module) **50**
rubric: Historic Garment Analysis Project **62**; for read the label assignment 77; research presentation **30**; world building (project) **196–199**

Said, E. W. 57
Saint Mary's University of Minnesota 72
School of Theatre at CalArts 42
Schwartz, H. 78
self-reflection 55, 69, 75, 78, 94
Serkownek, E. 27–28
shared vocabulary, people- and place-based curriculum 88
Shaw, M. 56
shibori project 74
Shukla, P. 140
sleeveless upper garment from Peru *106*
Snyder, A. 37
Sorensen-Unruh, C. 129
square-cut garment 108
standards-based grading (SBG) 122
St. Clair, K. 28

student-facing statement 169
student responses, abridged clothing history 119
style 7–22; analysis 19–20; course description 7–12; history of **8–10**; object-based approach 17–18; re-fashioning time 18–21; research 12–15, 19–20; sample assignment 13; synthesis 19–20; visual literacy 16–17
syllabus calendar **26–27**; abridged clothing history **113–117**; conscious fashion history **38–39**; cultural connections **124–125**; dress, history of **50–54**; issues of history **177–181**; people- and place-based curriculum **85–88**; undergraduate general education **75–76**

Tazewell, P. 59
Teaiwa, T. 20
technology, world building project 195
30%, Final Fashion History Paper (2,500-word essay) 41
Thompson, R. 56, 59
Tisch School of the Arts (New York University) 173
tools, multi-use 202
traditional cultural expressions (TCEs) 167
tunics: African *105*; Checkerboard Tunic *30*, 31; semi-fitted 108, *108*
20%, Group Study Project: The Renaissance/World-Building Exercise 41

Ulysses (Joyce) 175
undergraduate general education 71–82; advice on 80–81; Bachelor of Arts undergraduate program 81; learning objectives 74; learning outcomes 74–75; process involved in creation of the course 78–80; reasons for adapting 72–75; reflections on the undergraduate program 81–82; rubric for "read the label" assignment 77; syllabus calendar **75–76**
Ungrading (Blum) 123
University of Hawai'i, Mānoa 83–84, *89*
University of Massachusetts, Boston 140–141, 143
University of Michigan 157

Vanessa Lattas, 2022 *187–189*, 187–190
Verdugo Hills High School 102
visual literacy, style 16–17

Welters, L. 27, 40, 49, 71
Wendt, A. 99
Western fashion history 140–154; assignments **146–150**, 151; course description 140–141; course outcomes 144; experiential learning 152–154; reason behind evolution of the course 142–143; reflections 154; weekly schedule **144–145**
Wilkinson, M. 59
Williams, T. 68
Windsor, L. 37
world building project 191–199; assignment 192–193; course description 191–192; learning outcomes 191; room sketch for *194*; rubric **196–199**; technology 195; University of Utah 191–192
WorldCat 37
worn history project 184–190; *see also* personal history through clothes

Zai, R. 110

Taylor & Francis eBooks

www.taylorfrancis.com

A single destination for eBooks from Taylor & Francis with increased functionality and an improved user experience to meet the needs of our customers.

90,000+ eBooks of award-winning academic content in Humanities, Social Science, Science, Technology, Engineering, and Medical written by a global network of editors and authors.

TAYLOR & FRANCIS EBOOKS OFFERS:

- A streamlined experience for our library customers
- A single point of discovery for all of our eBook content
- Improved search and discovery of content at both book and chapter level

REQUEST A FREE TRIAL
support@taylorfrancis.com

For Product Safety Concerns and Information please contact our EU
representative GPSR@taylorandfrancis.com
Taylor & Francis Verlag GmbH, Kaufingerstraße 24, 80331 München, Germany

www.ingramcontent.com/pod-product-compliance
Lightning Source LLC
Chambersburg PA
CBHW081153290426
44108CB00018B/2530